COSMOLOGY

THE MACMILLAN COMPANY
NEW YORK · BOSTON · CHICAGO · DALLAS
ATLANTA · SAN FRANCISCO

MACMILLAN & CO., LIMITED
LONDON · BOMBAY · CALCUTTA
MELBOURNE

THE MACMILLAN CO. OF CANADA, LTD.
TORONTO

COSMOLOGY

A Text for Colleges

BY

J. A. McWILLIAMS, S.J.

New York
THE MACMILLAN COMPANY
1928

Nihil Obstat

ARTHUR J. SCANLAN, S.T.D.,

Censor Librorum.

Imprimatur

✠ PATRICK CARDINAL HAYES,

Archbishop, New York.

New York, April 19, 1928.

SET UP BY BROWN BROTHERS LINOTYPERS
PRINTED IN THE UNITED STATES OF AMERICA
BY THE FERRIS PRINTING COMPANY

INTRODUCTION

THE term "Cosmology" is derived from the word κόσμος (cosmos) by which the Greeks signified the visible world. Cosmology is therefore a study of the material universe; although the name was coined in comparatively recent times, the study itself is as old as philosophy and in the beginning constituted almost the entire scope of philosophical endeavor. Even after the broader philosophical development inaugurated by Socrates, cosmology continued to bulk large in the various systems. For centuries, at first among the Arabian philosophers and afterwards in the Christian schools of the Middle Ages, the wide observation and deep acumen of Aristotle were relied upon almost implicitly as the basis of cosmological discussions; still here and there, as in the case of Albertus Magnus and Roger Bacon, men were found who had immediate recourse to Nature herself in order to discover her secrets. With the resurgence of scientific investigation in the fifteenth century new conclusions were arrived at which upset those of the older physical science and so perplexed the philosophers as to occasion their retirement from the field of cosmology properly so called. The extreme of that retirement was at a later period strikingly exemplified in such idealistic philosophies as those of Schelling and Hegel. On the other hand, Aristotelian philosophers, and especially those of the more recent scholastic revival, have bravely essayed to harmonize the findings of science in a true and consistent philosophy of nature.

Cosmology may be defined as *a study of the general characteristics and basic principles of the material universe.* Cosmology differs from the physical sciences not in its material object (which, being the material universe, is the same for both) but in its formal object. By this last is meant that while the particular sciences set certain limits to their inquiry, philosophy recognizes no limits either as to the extent or the profundity of its investigations. Thus cosmology brings within its purview all material substance, whether ponderable or imponderable, living or non-living. In the present treatise corporeal life as such is omitted as being capable of more successful discussion in psychology, but living bodies are in every other respect within the scope of cosmology. The four causes (efficient, final, formal and material) are investigated with the purpose of carrying the inquiry as far as may be possible to unaided human reason. While in the pursuit of this object the most reliable data of recent science are laid under contribution, cosmology, as a special branch of philosophy, must not degenerate into a purely scientific treatise; nor, on the contrary, must it merge into general metaphysics, or ontology.

Gratitude is due for assistance from many eminent cosmologists too numerous for special mention. As will be clear to those conversant with the literature of the subject, the works of H. Schaaf and J. Donat have suggested the manner of treating certain questions.

CONTENTS

PART I
THE UNIVERSE IN GENERAL

vii

PART II
ON THE COMMON PROPERTIES OF BODIES

SECTION 1
EXTENSION, OR INTEGRAL COMPOSITION

CONTENTS

PART II

THE COMMON PROPERTIES OF BODIES

SECTION 2

ACTIVITY

PART III
THE SPECIFIC PROPERTIES OF BODIES

PART IV
THE ESSENTIAL COMPOSITION OF BODIES

PART I

THE MATERIAL UNIVERSE
IN GENERAL

COSMOLOGY

CHAPTER I

THE MAGNITUDE OF THE UNIVERSE

WHAT CONSTITUTES THE UNIVERSE. By the material universe is understood the sum total of all bodies that exist, the whole of extant corporeal substance. For our present purpose it is a sufficient description of this universe to state that it is made up of fixed stars and their attendant satellites, together with the ether of interstellar space. We are not to understand by the term "fixed star" that the body in question is altogether stationary, for we know that many such stars are moving through space at considerable speed, and we assume that all of them are in some kind of local motion. But a fixed star is one that is not moving in an orbit around a larger body. A satellite does so move, and with reference to it the larger body is considered stationary. Thus the sun in our planetary system is a fixed star, though together with its family of planets it is moving through space at the rate of many miles per second.

THE NUMBER OF STARS. Whether other fixed stars have satellites we do not know from observation, because of their great distance from us; but by analogy with our solar system we conclude that many of the fixed stars are centers of planetary systems.

When we consider that there are between six and seven thousand such stars visible to the naked eye we begin to have some notion of the size of our universe. But when we learn that the greater telescopes reveal many thousands of times the number of stars that are perceived by our unaided vision, and that by means of the one hundred inch mirror on Mount Wilson a photographic plate can be made to record very many more still, the very number of the stars surpasses our imagination. By this last mentioned process the conclusion has been reached that the stars which stud the heavens range in multitude from one to two thousand millions.

STELLAR DISTANCES. But scarcely less astonishing than the number of stars is their tremendous distance from one another. Although it takes four hours for the light of the sun to reach the outermost of its planets, Neptune, it takes the same light four years to reach the nearest fixed star, Alpha Centauri. The brightest fixed star in our firmament, Sirius, is nine light-years away. Betelgeuse, a mere point of light in the telescope, has a diameter of four hundred million miles. But distance becomes a mere enumeration in arithmetical characters when stars are said to be two hundred thousand, and even a million light-years away.

"INFINITE" EXTENT. In view of these estimates made by astronomers as to the size of our universe, it will not be necessary in our argument to prove that the extent is very great; for it must be conceded that the enormous expanse of the material world exceeds anything that we can really picture to our minds. But what we directly state in the thesis is that this extent somewhere has an end, that it is not without any termination whatsoever. We must be careful to distinguish the "infinity" of mathematics from that expressed in our thesis. In mathematics "infinity" means a quantity greater than any definite quantity you may choose to mention. Such a quantity is *indefinitely large,* but not actually infinite. The concept of *actual infinity* is not employed in mathematics. Actually infinite extension means (if indeed the term be not a contradiction) that there exists *in fact* a body, or bodies, which simply have no outer boundary or limit whatsoever. The indefinitely large quantity referred to in mathematics does not suppose that there are existing bodies whose extent exactly equals that quantity, or that there are existing beings whose number corresponds to it; because existing beings are definite in size and number, whereas the "infinity" of mathematics is always indefinite.[1]

THE QUESTION OF NUMBER. We are here concerned directly with the attribute of extension only, and not with any other properties of bodies. We cannot however escape the question of number. For in a world of actually infinite extent there would have to be either one body, or an actually infinite number of bodies. Because, if any one body were actually infinite in extent, there could not conceivably be room for any other; and if no one body were actually infinite in extent, then every one of them must be finite; and no matter how large each and every one might be, their sum could not result in an

---

[1] Cf. Aristotle *Metaph.* XI. 8. "There is no infinite magnitude in existence."

actually infinite extent except from an *actually infinite number* of them.

OPPONENTS OF THE THESIS. Certain Materialistic writers, e.g., Bückner, Haeckel, and others
explicitly contradict our thesis, holding as they do
that there is no beginning or end of the world in
space, that the world is simply unlimited, and that
there is no such thing as vacant space anywhere—
not outside the universe, for there could be no outside to such a world; not within the universe, for
that, too, would be a limitation and a boundary.
These men draw their conclusions from the assumption that the world is self-sufficient, or "divine" if
you will, and *a se*. We shall deal with that assumption in Thesis 5.

*Thesis 1. The extent of the material universe,
though very great, is not actually infinite*

Argument 1. There is no argument to show that
the world is *de facto* actually infinite in extent. But
in the absence of such argument the world cannot
rationally be said to be of such extent. Therefore ...

The major. We do not dispute that the conclusion of the Materialists may be correctly drawn
from their premise that the world is self-existent,
a se; but they do not offer a proof for the premise,
they only assert it. And since they hold that all
knowledge is limited to observation and experiment,
both the premise and the conclusion is clearly beyond the reach of knowledge for them. Besides
we shall see in a subsequent thesis that there can be
no rational contention that the world is *a se*.

The minor. The concept of actually infinite ex-

tension is so impossible to us and bristles with so
many apparent contradictions that to accept it as a
fact without proof is unreasonable.   Moreover
bodies are so finite and limited in other ways that
it is entirely gratuitous to assert that they are infinite in extent.

Argument 2. What is contradictory in itself is
false; but the assertion that the material universe
is actually infinite in extent is contradictory in itself.
Therefore . . .

The minor. In any *extension* we can conceive a
part to be subtracted, annihilated, or removed from
consideration.   Now the remainder is either finite
or infinite.   If finite, then that finite remainder plus
the finite part removed equaled infinity; which is
a contradition.   If the remainder be infinite, then the
void left by the part subtracted constitutes a limit
to the infinite remainder; and by restoring the part
we add to the actually infinite: all of which is
contradictory.

It also follows from the above that the universe
need not be considered as one body.   But, as we
have seen, if the number is plural at all it must be
actually infinite in order to make up a universe of
infinite extent.   And *an actually infinite number,* as
distinguished from the "infinite" of mathematics,
cannot be understood except as incapable of increase.
But the multitude of bodies is increased by the simple division of any one of them.   Or, to view the
matter in a slightly different way, extension, e.g., of
a line, cannot by any conceivable sort of division
be reduced to points.[2]   A reduction of points would

[2] Cf. Thesis 6.

indeed be the end of division, for since points cannot be divided, division could go no further; but to
suppose such an ending as possible or conceivable
would destroy the whole notion of extension. Hence
an end to division of extension is a contradiction.
But only at the end of division should we have an
actually infinite number. Therefore such a number
is a contradiction. And since a universe of infinite
extent involves the possibility of such a number,
such a universe is impossible in concept.

Difficulties. 1. Absolute space is infinite.
Reply. Absolute space is not a real being. As a creation
of the mind it represents indefinitely great expanse, the
infinitude of mathematics.

2. If the world were finite it should be enclosed by empty
space, i.e., by nothingness; but nothingness cannot enclose
something. (Kant.)
Reply. The world is not enclosed actually by anything
beyond its own boundaries, though we so *picture* it, e.g., in a
sea of space.

3. If the universe has boundaries the light of the stars
must eventually reach those boundaries, and since it can go
no farther, must be reflected back, with the result that we
should be able to see mirrored images of the stars.
Reply. Some have held that many of the so called fixed
stars are nothing more than such mirrored images. It is not
necessary to accept that opinion, for the objection supposes
that the boundaries are relatively near, whereas they may
be ever so remote without being actually infinite. Moreover
the amount of light from a mirror millions of light-years
away would be too faint to be perceived. In addition to this
the objection supposes that light itself is in no way diminished
by any amount of travel through the ether. That cannot
be proved. It is quite possible that some quantity of the

light may be converted into other forms of energy even in the ether of space. Again the objection overlooks the presence of other bodies, obscure or luminous, which must prevent a great portion of the light from successfully making the entire trip to the outer boundary and back to us. In any case its reflection back to a point on the earth would depend on its angle of incidence at the outer boundary of the universe; unless that boundary be very even and regular no image at all could be formed.

On the Probability of Inhabitants in Parts of the Universe Other than the Earth

WHERE? Philosophers and astronomers from the days of ancient Greece down to our own time have regarded it as probable that the entire race of men is not confined to the earth. Zenophanes, Anaxagoras, Galileo, Kepler, Newton, Secchi, Proctor, Mendive, Pohle are but a few of the many who have considered it probable that other parts of the universe are inhabited. The question is a scientific one to the extent of determining that the conditions requisite for human life are present. Beyond that it becomes a purely philosophical question. No one holds, of course, that there is life on any of the self-luminous, incandescent stars. But there are many obscure bodies in the heavens, and many of the fixed stars may have planets like our own. Some have attempted to make out a strong case for Mars; still the more conservative opinion is that the temperature of that planet is too low for life, as we know it, to propagate; and that thus the planet is beyond the stage at which it might have been inhabited. The planet Venus, covered as it appears to be with dense clouds which sunlight could scarcely penetrate, may be passing through that period which for the earth just preceded the dawn of life. But it is not at all necessary that we confine our speculations to the solar system.

OTHER RATIONAL ANIMALS? Revelation, intended as it is for terrestrial men, is generally conceded to be altogether silent on the question of rational inhabitants in other parts of the material universe. And when philosophical arguments for the affirmative are advanced it must not be thought that such arguments suppose men elsewhere to be in every respect like ourselves. They need only be rational animals. They need not have the same senses as we; they might have more than five, or less, or altogether different senses. They might be without sex, and the manner of propagation be altogether different from that of our race, if indeed there be propagation at all. They need not be bipeds, and might have means of locomotion totally unknown to us. The only thing that philosophers seek to establish is that there should be elsewhere in the universe beings who qualify as rational animals—that there have been in the past, are now, or will be in the future.

ARGUMENTS. The arguments, which admittedly cannot establish the point with certainty, may be summed up as follows. Other cosmic bodies seem to pass through the same cycles of evolution as the earth; and if life appeared at a certain stage of the earth's development, why did it not elsewhere? Reason shrinks from the thought that outside our little earth nothing but utter death reigns throughout the vast spaces of the universe and through all its ages. Moreover, since there are great varieties of irrational creatures, there is no objection to supposing varieties of rational animals. Add to this that better line of argument founded on the purpose of creation. Creation cannot have a rational purpose without including intelligent beings who are to know their Creator. Now the material world is not an adequate and proper object of cognition for spiritual creatures, but for rational animals. The immediate purpose of the creation of the material universe is that it be known by men, that through it they may know the Creator. But terrestrial men have an extremely sketchy knowledge of any of the cosmos beyond the earth. We can, it is true, suspect much that lies beyond our ken, and so have inklings of the greatness and resourcefulness of the Creator's power, but it seems extravagant to suppose that such a lavish outpouring of creatures should have as its sole object the stirring of conjectures in us who are inhabitants of the earth. Also, a certain feeling of comfort and satisfaction with the work of God arises from the thought that there may be elsewhere races of men who give more honor to the Creator than is the case here on our earth. The mercy of God is indeed glorified in our regard; still there are other attributes of the Creator that could well be more becomingly honored than they are by terrestrial mankind. So, too, those who would belittle the importance of man in the universe by reviling him with the reminder that his habitat is but a tiny speck of dust, may find reason to consider that even that jeer of theirs is wide of the mark, for man may inhabit many other portions of the universe as well. That jeer is, as G. K. Chesterton says, an attempt "to shame spirituality with size," but we might also ask these insulters of mankind to prove that man's dwelling is after all confined to earth. There is a still further resort by appealing to the resurrection; however, the Scholastic school usually holds that the resurrection is in no way due to man's nature, and so excludes it from the scope of philosophy. In philosophy we consider that the visible creation is intended for man's life on this side of the grave. It is true that even in regard to the earth itself man has not as yet attained an exhaustive knowledge of it, but he is in a better position to study it than he is to sound the wonders of nature in some sphere at the remotest reaches of space. The proposition that these regions may be better known by other men, is, therefore, surely not opposed to right reason.

Topics for Discussion. How astronomers calculate stellar distances. Mathematical infinity. The conditions necessary for organic life. The "canals" on Mars.

REFERENCES

Cath. Ency. "The Universe." "Infinity."

Irish Eccl. Record, Vols. 12, 13. "Is Our Earth Alone Inhabited?"

Winchell, A. *Reconciliation of Science and Religion,* p. 373. *Sketches of Creation* (Univ. of Michigan, 1874), Chs. 4, 40.

CHAPTER II

TELEOLOGY

PURPOSE. Purpose, or *end,* is that for the sake of which a thing is done, or for which it is fit or apt. An end is something *good,* either for self or others (*bonum sibi vel aliis*). Hence an end is always in some respect desirable. Thus, though study be irksome, it may still be desirable in view of the advantages to be gained. When a thing is sought for no desirability of its own, but only in reference to some good to be derived from it, it becomes simply a *means* to an end. But if, besides being a means to some further good, it is also desired for its own sake, it is called a *proximate end.* Health, for instance, is desirable in itself, and furthermore may be a means of earning a living. An *ultimate end* is one that is not referred to any other.

INTENTIONAL FITNESS. In the mind the end precedes the action which it dictates; it is then called the *end intended.* In external fact the end follows the action as its result; it is then called the *end obtained.* The opponents of our thesis concede that ends are obtained in the universe; what they are loath to admit is that these ends are intended. That these ends are intended is what we wish to demonstrate in the first part of our proof. By "purposive finality" we therefore mean an activity or fitness of things is dictated by the ends to be obtained. Once that is admitted, the second part of the thesis follows logically. One is tempted to think that it is a dislike for the second part that has prompted many savants to quarrel with the first part.

SCOPE OF THE THESIS. By the term "material universe" we signify the sum total of natural objects, i.e., bodies, living and non-living, as they occur in nature; but we exclude the particular constructions into which the forces of nature are thrown by the art of man, such as machines, houses, highways, etc. Man cannot introduce new forces into nature, but he can employ those he finds there in new combinations to produce results which without the intervention of man would not occur. Such combinations are technically called *artificial,* as opposed to natural objects; and they are excluded from consideration in our thesis, since they are too evidently fashioned with purposive finality to occasion any dispute.

COÖPERATION. The proximate, or immediate, ends for which natural objects are apt are many and multifarious according to the nature of the countless kinds of bodies that make up the universe. Although we do not pretend to know all these ends, we know enough of them to establish our thesis with certainty. And we are warranted in concluding, with scientific men generally, that every natural object has some function or use. Still it is not strictly necessary for the verity of the thesis that every natural object without exception have a natural purpose, peculiar to it. Furthermore we consider both intrinsic and extrinsic purpose. The *intrinsic end,* or purpose, of a being is that which is good for itself, or at least for its species; it is the *bonum sibi.* A being's very nature is primarily constituted to fulfill this intrinsic purpose. Thus a grain of wheat is primarily fitted to produce other wheat, and meanwhile to preserve itself in that aptitude. The *extrinsic end* is the good which a being can contribute to other beings; it is the *bonum aliis.* A very notable extrinsic end of the grain of wheat is to serve as food for man. It is by means of extrinsic ends that the world is linked together into an ordered system, or cosmos. The interrelation and coöperation thus brought about among the multitudinous parts of the universe have so many ramifications, from the grandest scale to the most minute, that a book would be required even to sketch them in outline. Suffice it to mention here three grand divisions of this coöperation. The mineral, or inorganic, kingdom is fitted to minister to plant-life. Plants, together with some inorganic substance, as water and air, not to mention the conveyors of light and heat, perform an indispensable service to the life of animals. And the service is mutual, as in the case of the bee and the moth with regard to flowers. It would be easy, too, to show how all the visible universe is serviceable to man in his intellectual life, but the whole subject is too vast to do more than touch upon it here. This coöperation of parts was so patent even to the ancient Greeks with their imperfect knowledge of science that their word for world, cosmos, was the same as that for order.

THE ORDER OF NATURE AND THE COURSE OF

NATURE. *Order* is the harmonious coöperation of many members unto the same end. If the coöperation of a small group of beings, or of the members of a single being, be referred to, the order is called *particular*. If world order be referred to, it is called *universal order*. The latter is also divided into the order of nature and the course of nature. *The order of nature* is the particular setting at any given moment, and consists especially in this: (1) That matter has certain forces which serve to maintain each being in its specific entity, and, besides (2) certain properties which are serviceable to others; (3) that there is a sufficient quantity of each kind to provide an ordered coöperation; (4) that the various kinds and quantities of matter are so placed or collocated with respect to one another as to result in an ordered universe instead of chaos; and (5) that the different affinities or "appetites" of the countless bodies in the universe are such as to produce a long and continuous series of ordered events. This series of events is called the *course of nature*. The tremendous advance of science has done nothing more than to reveal this interrelation and mutual coöperation of the parts, however minute or great, of the physical world.

EFFICIENT AND FINAL CAUSES. In discussing purposive finality it is very important accurately to determine the state of the question. A final cause does not deny nor does it exclude efficient cause; on the contrary, the final supposes the efficient; evidence of both is discernible in the same phenomenon. *Efficient cause* is that which produces an effect by its own physical activity, as when the wind disturbs the sea, or turns a mill. A man building a house is the efficient cause of the edifice; but there is clearly another cause at work here, it is his wages. The money itself which the man expects is not driving any nails or lifting bricks, still these things would not be done without the money in view. *Final cause,* then, is the end intended, the good desired. Final cause induces the efficient cause to act and directs the action along definite lines. It is *that for the sake of which a thing is done.* Thus, when a man walks, the efficient cause of the walking is a certain group of muscles in the body; but the good in view, e.g., getting home, is accountable for the rise of the activity and the direction of its course. The influence of both causes is discernible in the one objective fact. It should not be necessary to labor this point were it not that some writers pretend that the two causes are mutually exclusive, that there is only an alternative choice; then grandly espousing efficient cause they indignantly reject the final. The true question is not "efficient or final," but whether besides efficient cause, which is not in dispute here, there is also final cause as a necessary explanation of the universe as we know it.

NECESSITY IN THE IMMEDIATE AGENT. Another point to be made clear is that which concerns freedom and necessity. We admit that in order that the influence of final cause may be had, there must be an intelligent being to whom the end in view may appeal, and who may direct activities toward that end. And an intelligent being is conceded also to be a free being. But the freedom does not have to be in each and every being that is acting with purposive finality. A watchmaker is a free being, but in putting the parts of a watch together he is dealing with forces that are unfree, that act necessarily in a fixed and determined manner; still the whole watch displays purposive finality. The unfree agent carries out the freely chosen purpose of the maker. Hence, in our thesis we do not deny that *natural objects act necessarily*, but we assert that their activities and their very make-up are evidence of final causality.

INTELLIGENCE. Much less is it necessary that the immediate agent *know* the purpose of its nature or its activities. Only beings with intelligence can recognize a purpose as such. A brute animal eats its food without recognizing that the purpose of food is to sustain life. The intelligence which a bird displays in building its nest is an intelligence which the bird itself does not possess. In place of intelligence it has an instinctive impulse, or "urge." This inclination, or nisus, of a natural agent toward that which is good for it or its species is called *appetite* or *innate tendency*. *"Merely natural appetite"* is that of a being which is incapable of any cognition whatever, namely, it is the inclination or aptitude for certain functions of the inorganic or vegetative orders. Appetite attended with cognition is called *elicited;* and this in turn is *sensitive appetite* if the cognition of the good craved is merely sense cognition; it is *rational appetite* if the cognition is intellectual. Only in the case of the last named does the immediate agent recognize purpose as such.

History of the Question. The discussion of final activity, or teleology, is as old as philosophy itself. On the affirma-

tive side are Anaxagoras, Plato, Aristotle, the Fathers of
the Church, the Scholastic philosophers, Copernicus, Kepler,
Newton, Boyle, and countless others. In the dissenting
group are found Democritus and Epicurus, who admitted
only efficient causality; Francis Bacon and Descartes who
brush the question aside as not being a scientific one (these
men are in no true sense opponents of the thesis) ; Spinoza,
whose Pantheism admits only absolute necessity in the
totality of being, and who chooses on that supposition to
deny finality; Kant, who can get no further than subjective
conviction; Darwinians of the atheistic type (Darwin himself in the last paragraph of the *Origin of Species* lauded
the teleology of creation) ; the Materialists and Naturalists
generally.

Modern science, especially in its investigations of the
functions of organs and the instinctive impulses of animals,
has supplied abundant material with which the philosopher
may establish and illustrate his thesis on the teleology of
nature. And, while scientists, as is their right within their
sphere, usually prescind from the question of intended purpose, some agnostic savants go out of their way explicitly to
deny purpose. The latter generally indulge in the fallacy
of ignoring the state of the question; this is clear from the
fact that they give such puerile reasons as that an organ acts
necessarily under given conditions, or that an animal does
not know the motive of its instinctive impulse. These
things are not denied by those who hold purposive finality,
for they are not incompatible with it. For some time
teleology was stigmatized, by such writers, with the pon-
derous name of "anthropomorphism," as though we made
out that God seeks His objectives in the tentative and
imperfect manner of men. More recently they are wont to
confess that things do act "as if" there were ends—*als ob*—
without admitting that the end has anything to do with the
manner of activity. Briefly, these men refuse to go beyond

the material universe for any explanation of that universe, and prefer to accept a blind, inexorable, corporeal idol which they call "Nature," as a primal postulate of their philosophy, instead of the intelligent extramundane Divinity to Whose existence the human mind easily and normally concludes so long as it does not begin by imposing barriers which it shall not cross.

Thesis 2. The material universe displays purposive finality, for which the ultimate reason must be sought in a supramundane intelligent cause of the world's order

Part I

Argument 1. Those things must be said to act for a purpose which act in the same evident manner as we do when we act for a purpose. But natural agents act in the same manner, and even more perfectly than we do when conscious purpose governs our action. Therefore natural agents must be said to act for a purpose.

The major. Each of us is most frequently conscious of an end in view, and is aware that his actions originate, continue and are controlled by the end in view. That is a personal experience, and it expresses what we mean by "purposive finality." Now, when I see other men acting in a like manner, I at once conclude, without their telling me, that they are prompted and governed by purposes. Moreover, when I discover the products of human art, as for instance in the excavations at Pompeii, I am forced to conclude that human activities were aroused and directed by certain ends they had in view: for example, to make a chariot wheel, a grist-

mill, a water-trough for horses, a cooking-utensil,
to build a street or a house, etc. I know that purpose governed the activities which produced these
things. And how do I know that? Not from any
human testimony, for none has survived. I know
it from the sheer aptitude of the things produced,
from their fitness for certain uses. Such apt results
could not occur unless *intended*.

Another line of reflection may be outlined thus.
I breathe the air about me with an insuperable impulse; and when I discover that air is necessary for
bodily life I cannot but conclude that the impulse
to breathe is for the purpose of supplying the
organism with what is necessary for its life. The
same is true of the appetite for food, and of other
bodily appetites: I can determine their purpose not
only for men but for brute animals; and by following out the same evidence of inclination and aptitude
I am forced to extend my conclusion to vegetative
life and the mineral kingdom as well. There are
unconscious tendencies in myself, as evidenced by
the incessant beating of the heart and the processes
of digestion, and I learn the purpose from the results. Likewise, in the case of a deliberate act,
when I have totally forgotten it and its purpose, I
can rediscover that purpose by noticing the thing
done, as when I see a whistle I made as a boy, or a
sharpened pencil lying on my desk. Hence if I
cannot know what is expressed in the major of the
argument, there is nothing I can know.

The minor. Not much need be said here. To
take but one example from among millions, the
acorn builds an oak with greater order and more

exquisite adaptation of means to an end than even a man builds a house. Responding to warmth and moisture the acorn sends out roots by which it selects from the soil the particular nourishment it needs; it builds up a trunk and branches with leaves which with the aid of light extract the proper substances from the air; it renews the leaves, and produces other acorns that are able to repeat the process. In fact the study of nature simply reveals to us such aptitudes and adaptations of means to an end.

Therefore the material universe in a most overwhelming way displays purposive finality.

Argument 2. Natural agents by the most complicated processes produce a very detailed and ordered result beneficial to the agent. We need only instance the act of seeing. But such activity can be explained only by purposive finality, namely, only on the ground that some intelligence intended that result. Therefore natural agents display purposive finality.

The major is evident, and admitted by all.

The minor. (a) There is no other sufficient cause, as is acknowledged by the conviction of all mankind in much simpler effects. Let a man but discover on some lone island a crude tomahawk or a sundial, and no amount of argument will persuade him that these things were the product of unreasoning nature. The human mind recognizes an essential connection between fitness and intention.

(b) Our experience also warrants the conviction that a highly complicated order cannot result otherwise than from intelligent direction. One might by means of colored pebbles construct on the beach a mosaic of the landscape before him, but on the strength of his experience he would never expect the winds and waves to do it for him. Yet every eye regularly represents what is before it, even the most shifting scenes. And if the ordered performances of the eye are worthy of years of study, what shall we say of the order throughout the universe from atom to solar system?

(c) Moreover, the order in the universe does not happen just once, as might be said of a still picture. There is constant change in every instant of time, and always there is order preserved in all the mutations and developments. To attempt to explain such progressive results, achieved by astounding coördination and coöperation of the constituent elements, without having recourse to an intelligent cause is to stultify the human mind.

(d) The appeal to the inexorable necessity of the world processes merely distracts the attention from the thing to be explained, namely, that they are *ordered* processes whatever their necessity.

Part II

Argument. The material universe gives evidence of intelligence as the cause of its order. But this cause is not the world itself. Therefore it is extramundane.

The major was proved in part one.

The minor. The natural objects under discussion do not recognize ends as such, and consequently are not themselves intelligent. Man, in his deliberate acts, is indeed exempted from the discussion; but no one holds that man is accountable for the world's order.

Note. This does not prove that the Author of the world's order is absolutely infinite, but it proves that He is superior to the world and distinct from it, and omnipotent at least to the extent that He is more powerful than all the forces of the material universe, since He established them and put them in order.

Difficulties. 1. The end does not exist until the action is done. But what does not exist until the action is done cannot be a motive for the action.

Reply. The end is not obtained in external fact until the action is done, I grant; the end does not exist in the mind as something intended before the action is done, I deny.

2. The world is ruled by chance. An oak, e.g., will produce thousands of acorns in vain compared to the few that may grow into other oaks.

Reply. Even granting that none of the acorns ever grow into an oak, it is clear that they are fitted to do so, and hence manifest finality; the oak is thus producing by the thousands concrete arguments for our thesis. Moreover the acorns are serviceable as food for animals and for enriching the soil for further vegetation; they are fit not only for the *bonum sibi,* but *bonum aliis* as well. This inter-service of the parts of the universe gives us still more overwhelming evidence of finality. And even confining our consideration to the primary end of propagation of the species, the tremendous insistence of nature that nothing shall thwart that end is all the more emphasized by the prolific profusion of seeds. If you demand a simpler means of obtaining the end, you are criticizing the wisdom of the Author of nature, but you are in no degree casting out the evidence of intelligence. On the other hand, the prodigality, so called, of nature might easily be justified on the sole ground of manifesting to man the liberality of the Creator.

3. In living beings there are many rudimentary organs that are entirely useless; e.g., the vermiform appendix, the eyes of the mole, the muscles for moving the human ear, etc.

Reply. We might grant that these structures have no purpose whatsoever, and never had any, nor ever will have, without in the least infringing the argument for finality. There is so overpowering an abundance of evidence for purpose that we do not need these few remnants as though they were indispensable to the argument. Were we proving that the Author of nature is infinitely wise, we might, perhaps, be called upon to explain some such apparent discrepancies. The objection attempts to ignore the point at issue, which is not whether God be absolutely infinite in His wisdom, and whether in such case He might produce apparently useless things; the question is whether He is endowed with intelligence, or entirely without it. As a matter of fact the manifest order of the world is too great for us ever to sound the depths of the Intelligence responsible for it. The more we investigate the more astoundingly the marvels of order open to our view. The fact that we have not as yet discovered the purpose of a natural object is no sign that it has none. Even now the medical profession is discovering purposes of the appendix. Also the uniformity of structural design is an evidence of intelligence in the Maker, just as the aptitude to reproduce that structure is an evidence of finality in the natural agent. Briefly, the difficulty is wide of the mark; and although it hit the mark it has no force.

4. Science follows the principle of closed causality, i.e., not to seek outside the world for an explanation of things in the world. But such a principle excludes an extramundane cause of the world's order.

Reply. The scope of physical science is to discover the

integral parts of bodies and to formulate the laws of their activities; hence it is not called upon to give any explanation beyond the statement that such and such is the nature of the bodies. Science takes nature as a datum, but if it be true science it does not condemn the philosophical attempt to explain nature. On the contrary scientific investigation supplies philosophy with abundant data from which to reason to an extramundane cause of the world's order. Thus science, whether willingly or not, becomes an *ancilla philosophiae*.

5. Out of all the combinations possible to chance the present world order is one. Therefore that order may be due to chance.

Reply. When we consider that there is order in each single atom, and molecule, and crystal, and cell, and organ, and organism, and in the interrelation of all the various classes of beings, and that there is coöperation to a refined degree among all the forms of energy, and when we reflect on the countless constituents of the material world, we begin to see how futile is the appeal to chance. But that is not all; the world is in a condition of constant change, and has been so, according to science, for millions of years. The astounding chance which the objection postulates for any given instant of that time, must be repeated all over again in every infinitesimal fraction of the world's duration; for order is preserved throughout the continuous change. Such an occurrence is mathematically and metaphysically impossible. The idea of its happening by chance even once makes the mind reel; but the infinite repetition of it in the steadily developing progress of events, without ever a slip, is too absurd for thought.

6. Given a certain amount of matter, equipped with certain forces, and granted that the matter thus diversified be distributed in the proper ratio and collocation, then all the physical and chemical processes which we recognize as world-

order follow *inevitably*. But the original condition might
happen by chance, i.e., without guiding intelligence. Therefore all the rest might happen without guiding intelligence.

Reply. Leaving aside the fact that the objection fails to
explain the presence of man's intelligence, and the supposition that the activities of organism are entirely reducible to
mechanics, we need only single out necessity as the point by
which this objection attempts to bolster up the preceding
one. This necessity is lodged in the forces. Thus narrowed
down the question must again be cleared of suppositions not
pertinent to the present subject. The objection pretends that
the doctrine of 'finality does not require necessity in the
natural agent. On the contrary, however, finality does
require necessity in the natural agent. Again, the
objection tacitly presumes that the ultimate atoms of
the universe are possessed of a necessity which they have
never received from another being. We grant the necessity
but object to the presumption of their not having received it,
since that presumption is a surreptitious intrusion of a
coveted conclusion within the premises. Furthermore the
objection assumes that an unimposed (*a se*) necessity can
itself be imposed upon and modified, as is constantly the case
with the forces of nature. But the objection's real weakness,
concealed under all these confusing assumptions, is that it is
silent on the exact point at issue, which is not the necessity,
nor yet the fact that the forces of nature are modified and
modify others in turn, but that they do so *in such a way*
that a very complicated and highly ordered universe results,
and continues unceasingly to result and to develop. That is
the fact which always stares us in the face, and from which
all the clamor about necessity (which no one denies) can
never distract our attention. Necessity is irrelevant; the
only thing which matters here is *aptitude* to produce these
results. That aptitude, both active and passive, is written
large over the face of the universe and down into its every

fiber, and by means of that aptitude the universe has arrived, through long and increasingly complicated achievements, at a most intricate and highly coördinated result before which science to-day stands amazed. Time but unfolds the order contained in the aptitude of the forces. The original "ratio and collocation" constitute the least part of the world's order, for it merely begins there. A far greater marvel is that the forces can develop *another* order from *any* given ratio and collocation, and continue to repeat the marvel through countless successions of changes. To ask that we grant all this aptitude as not due to intelligence reduces the objection to the following form: If you grant that the whole ordered course of nature is not due to intelligence, then it follows that the whole ordered course of nature is not due to intelligence.

7. Many things in nature are abhorrent, as pain, parasites, monstrosities, the struggle for existence, defects and evils of all sorts. But these things cannot be considered as intended.

Reply. Our task here is to show that the Author of the world is intelligent. We leave to theodicy the vindication of His wisdom and goodness. The things cited as examples give evidence of intelligence, whether they be pleasant or not.

Corollary. The extrinsic purpose of irrational beings is the good of man. This service rendered by irrational nature is in the last analysis the manifestation of the goodness of the Creator. It is intended that man profit by visible creation as a means of heightening his appreciation of that goodness. The intrinsic end or purpose of human nature is to possess true good and happiness; our nature is constituted with that objective in view. The possession of it is the fulfillment. In the conferring of this true good and happiness God finds His greater glory. That glory therefore is the ultimate extrinsic end of mankind.

The Origin of Matter

We have seen that God is the efficient cause of the world's order. Since the world's order includes not only the arrangement of the forces, but the very forces themselves, the Founder of the order originated the forces. If, however, all the forces, all the active properties, were to be removed from the world, what should be left? By removal is not meant the mere stopping of activity; for the forces are forces whether acting or not, and they are order whether acting or not. If anything should be left after the utter removal of all forces, it could be none other than pure and undiversified matter. Aristotle inclined to the view that such matter did exist previous to the introduction of forces. Many modern scientists are inclined to the opposite view that matter is not physically distinct from force. MacMillan, e.g., says, "Matter has disappeared, and only organization is left." If that means anything, it means that matter is physically indistinct from forces. In case you choose to identify matter with force, so that the two are physically inseparable, then to say that God instituted the order of the world is to say that He originated the world outright.

If you hold that matter is something physically distinct from the forces of nature, then you have still to determine the origin of the matter. Matter without forces were incapable of activity, and hence could never of itself begin activity; nor could it have any purpose in existence. We have seen moreover that the forces in matter were originated by the Founder of the world's order; hence matter is subject to Him, hence it is certainly not *a se,* and consequently is a *produced being*. One kind of production, the only kind we have immediate experience of, is the production of something new *in a given subject*. Even the originating of forces in matter (a thing which man cannot do) is production in a subject, namely in matter. But what of the subject? It also is produced; and it is the ultimate subject. Therefore it is produced without a previous subject, in other words without a material cause; that is *productio ex nihilo subjecti,* and is called *creation*. Creation is properly treated in theodicy, and it is sufficient to say here, that, since matter without forces could have no purpose, it was originated simultaneously with the forces of nature. And though this matter as such has no material cause, it has an efficient cause in the Creator; and together with the forces that organize it, it has a final cause.

The Pantheists hold that God produces the world out of His own substance, as the material cause. We reject that in Thesis 5.

Topics for Discussion. Reconciliation of the non-intelligence of irrational nature with its purposeful activity. The finality of instincts and adaptation in animals. The incompatibility of chance (as something essentially variable) with the necessity of physical laws. "Useless" organs. Unity of the universe. Aptitude of inorganic matter as the

key to world processes.   Physical and moral evils
compatible with a beneficent Creator.

REFERENCES

Ball, R. *The Story of the Heavens.*
Cath. Ency. "Final Cause." "God." "Cause." "Creation."
Cath. World, Vol. 119, p. 145. "Blind Chance or God."
Gerard, J. *Old Riddle and Newest Answer.*
Month, Vol. 113, p. 32. "Teleology."
Harris, C. *Pro Fide.*
    Creed or No Creed.
Hettinger, F. *Natural Religion.*
Houck, F. *Our Palace Wonderful* (Hansen & Sons,
    Chicago), Chs. 2, 3.
Ryan, J. H. *An Introduction to Philosophy,* Ch. 5.
Schanz, P. *A Christian Apology.*

CHAPTER III

INORGANIC EVOLUTION

COSMOGONIES. Cosmogony is any theory which professes to account for the way in which the world arrived at its present state of organization. We do not here espouse any particular theory, but merely assert that any theory which comes under the general description given in the statement of the thesis, far from being repugnant to philosophical reasoning, is rather in accord with the conclusions of sound philosophy. Nor must it be thought that evolution is opposed to creation; for evolution supposes something to evolve. And by confining our thesis to the inorganic world we avoid the current contention about the evolution of organic bodies. The older Scholastic philosophers by their acceptance of "spontaneous generation" held some instances of the genesis of life from non-life. That position was abandoned after the scientific investigations of Pasteur. But they also held evolution of the inorganic world, as may be seen, for example, in the statement of St. Thomas that "the earth was formerly in a potential state . . . its parts diffused." [1] St. Augustine and St. Gregory of Nyssa maintained that although God is distinctly the Author of life, He did not intervene at the point of time when life appeared, but in the very first instant of creation

[1] *De coelo*, L.27.

32

introduced those forces into matter which afterwards resulted in the various forms of life. All agree that the inorganic world developed by the action of forces introduced once and for all at the beginning. Hence, so far as there has been any reasoned opposition to the general notion of evolution, it has been directed against one or other particular theory, and has been rightly based on scientific grounds. At the dawn of Grecian philosophy we find the Ionians almost totally engrossed in the question of how the world developed from primordial matter, and even advancing theories of organic evolution, as Anaxamander did.

MODERN ADVANCES. For centuries the Ptolemaic system of astronomy held the field; it was a geocentric theory. In the sixteenth century, Copernicus, a cleric and physician as well as astronomer, got out the system that is accepted today: thus was fulfilled the conjecture of St. Thomas [2] that some day another system might supplant the Ptolemaic. After the Copernican system had been perfected by Kepler, Galileo, and Newton, the time was ripe for new cosmogonies. Kant and Laplace, independently of one another, suggested the hypothesis that the planets and their satellites, together with the sun, once formed a single igneous mass of varying density, that the denser portions became centers of attraction with the result that the entire mass began to rotate and certain parts separated out as planets, continuing their motion in the same sense as the original mass. This theory later gave way before the spiral-nebula explanation, which in turn is yield-

[2] *De coelo*, L.17; *Sum. th.* I, 32, a.2, ad.2.

ing ground to the Chamberlain-Moulton hypothesis. This latest conjecture is to the effect that our planetary system had its origin in the close approach of another heavenly body. The calculated result is that the strong attraction set up between the sun and the passing star, attended by internal disturbances within the sun itself, would cause the eruption of great portions of the sun's substance which afterwards formed themselves into planets. On this supposition, the uniform motion in the solar system is easily explained. The fact that several satellites of the outer planets have a retrograde movement, i.e., westward instead of eastward, can be accounted for on the assumption that they were stray bodies captured by these planets. The same assumption will hold for the rapidly moving satellite of Mars.

GEOGONY. Geogony is the study of the genesis of the earth. An abundance of data for this study is supplied by the sciences of geology, geophysics, and seismography. As the statement of our thesis indicates, there is much more evidence of the inorganic evolution of the earth than for the rest of the universe, the principal reason being that the evidence with regard to the earth is more accessible to us.

THE UNIVERSE AT LARGE. The presence of nebulæ in the heavens, as well as the different colors of the fixed stars, give some clue for conjectures about the process of formation outside the solar system. As contraction of the mass proceeds heat increases; contraction is ultimately retarded, and the heat is radiated off. There would seem thus to be a progression from the gigantic red star to the large yellow, to the white, to the smaller yellow, ending in the dwarf red star. The sun is considered to have reached the second stage of yellow.

THE POINT AT ISSUE. Whatever may be said for or against any cosmogonic hypothesis in particular, we are here concerned only with the underlying supposition that the universe has arrived at its present highly elaborate condition by the prolonged operation of forces inherent in matter itself. We take "evolution" in the broad sense of a natural process whereby a rudimentary condition develops into a more highly organized result. And we say that this course of nature is due to material forces *immediately*. By that we mean that the substances in the universe act with their own efficiency, and are not merely moved about like pawns by some higher power. At the same time we hold, pursuant to the previous thesis, that the ultimate determinant of the course of nature is the act of the Creator, Who instituted these forces in matter.

Thesis 3. On philosophical grounds there is no objection to admitting the evolution of the inorganic world, and especially of the earth, as immediately due to the agency of material forces: in fact, such process of formation is quite consonant with the attributes of the Creator

Part I (a) The universe in general

Argument. The two philosophical conclusions against which the general theory of inorganic evolu-

tion might conceivably militate are that the world
was created and that its order supposes intelligence
in its Maker.   But the general theory of inorganic
evolution does not militate against either of these
conclusions.   Therefore inorganic evolution is not
in conflict with philosophy.

The minor. Evolution takes place in matter and
by the forces of matter; therefore it *presupposes* the
existence of the material agents.   Hence it is far
from excluding creation.

The ordered progression and highly organized
results of evolution demand that the materials of
the universe be apt for such action, reaction and
adaptation as alone could produce such results; that
they be given in the proper proportion, and be
properly distributed in space with respect to one
another.   But all this is evidence of intelligence.
Therefore evolution, instead of excluding, postulates intelligence.

Part I (b) The earth in particular

Argument. Countless data demonstrate beyond
doubt that the earth's crust was gradually formed by
known forces of the inorganic world.   But philosophy would be captious to quarrel either with the
data or the conclusion.   Therefore philosophy can
find no reasonable ground for objecting to inorganic evolution of the earth.

The major.   The wealth of data supplied by
geology, supported as it is by paleontology, is sufficient to convince even the most desultory reader. To
mention only one phenomenon, igneous rock has
clearly erupted through the sedimentary strata and

these latter are buckled and faulted in such ways as to leave no doubt about the nature of the process. Moreover in the strata are found footprints of animals, partial and entire skeletons, marks of wounds sustained and even vestiges of food in the stomach.

The minor. It were folly to maintain that nature produced these things without going through the long processes which they indicate.

Part II. Such process is consonant with the attributes of the Creator

Argument. Such process of world formation as has been outlined exhibits effectively the wisdom, power, goodness, immensity and eternity of the Creator.

Wisdom in a high degree is revealed by accomplishing such complicated and intimately coördinated results from such simple beginnings; *power* by the release of such tremendous energy as was spent in bringing the world to its present state. The *goodness* also of the Creator is manifest not only in committing such a large share of coöperation to creatures, but likewise in the evidence of the long and laborious process by which the earth was prepared for the habitation of man. The *immensity* of God is forcibly suggested to the mind by the wide reaches of space over which His power holds sway; and His *eternity* by the indefinitely long eons through which these world processes have been going on.

Difficulties. 1. The world is either created or evolved; but it is evolved; therefore it is not created.[3]

[3] Cf. Haeckel, *Welträtsel*, c.13.

Reply. I deny that the disjunction of the major is correct; the one does not exclude the other—unless, indeed, "evolved" means that the world sprang from nothing without any cause whatever, that, viz., inconceivable absolute nothingness produced the world and its order. But if that absurdity is meant by "evolved," then certainly the minor cannot be proved from science, to which an appeal is made. (The question of an eternally evolving world, which is really Haeckel's assumption, is treated at the end of the next thesis.)

2. According to the book of Genesis the world was formed in six days. But such a short period is untenable in the light of science.

Reply. Since philosophy proves its thesis from reason, and not from revelation, which the opponents reject, a fair objection from those opponents cannot make an appeal to revelation. Otherwise the objection is entirely *ad hominem*. Nevertheless, in the present matter, it is well known that Christian antiquity did not understand the "days" of Genesis to be twenty-four hour periods, as is clear from the writings of St. Augustine and others.

Topics for Discussion. The spiral nebula hypothesis of the formation of the universe. The Chamberlain-Moulton hypothesis of the origin of our solar system. The inner structure of the earth as revealed by the science of seismology.

REFERENCES

America, Vol. 20, p. 523. "The Dogma of Evolution."
Cath. Ency. "Evolution."
Cath. World, Vol. 25, p. 90. "The Copernican Theory and Evolution."
Husslein, J. *Evolution and Social Progress,* Ch. 8.

Irish Eccl. Record, Vol. 13, p. 335. "Divine Revelation and the Nebular Theory."

Irish Theol. Quarterly, Vol. 15, p. 227. "Evolution and Creation."

Kinns, S. *Harmony of the Bible with Science.*

Molloy, G. *Geology and Revelation.*

More, L. *The Dogma of Evolution.*

Wagner, A. *Origin of Continents and Oceans.*

Windle, B. *The Church and Science,* Chs. 11, 12.

CHAPTER IV

THE RESULT OF ENTROPY

MEANING OF THE THESIS. It is not our contention in the thesis that the material of which the world is composed will cease to exist. With St. Thomas, we agree that "there is no substance which will be entirely reduced to nothingness." [1] That could happen only by annihilation. Nor do we hold that the forces of matter will be altogether extinguished and blotted out. But we assert that the conditions of light, heat and chemical activity which are necessary for corporeal life will not continue forever. On the other hand, we do not deny that God can or will restore the universe after it shall have run its natural course. We are concerned merely with the natural course of events, and not with any free intervention on the part of the Creator.

THE OPPOSITE THESIS. The material world from all available scientific evidence is, so to speak, running down. Its store of useful energy is constantly being used up, without any means of restoration in sight. It is true that many "energy pumps" have been devised, but none of them are warranted by the observed facts of nature. Some have resorted to the collision of heavenly bodies, as, e.g., Haeckel. Arrhenius, a Swedish scientist, thought he had

[1] *Sum. th.* I, q.104, a.4.

40

solved the problem by the near encounter of such
bodies. MacMillan in our own country makes a
"postulate" that atoms are being reconstructed
somewhere. These men take the ground that the
world is eternal, from that position they are determined never to recede, and it is confessedly the ultimate reason for the theories which they have con-
trived. Now, if the world shall come to an end, it
is certainly not eternal. On the other hand, if we
were to suppose, as these men do, that the world
is a perpetual motion machine, that fact would not
prove that the world *is* eternal. Motion of that
character is not inconceivable; and though it is impossible in a man-made machine, it is so because the
man-made machine is subject to the same law as
prevails throughout nature, namely, of using up
energy in doing work. But who will gainsay that
the Creator could have produced such a machine?
To prove our thesis, we have only to prove that the
world is *de facto* not perpetual; and we rely totally
on the data of science. Our opponents, to establish
their thesis, must abandon the data of science; and
even supposing that their theories be true, they have
in no way established their conclusion that the world
is eternal. Much less may they conclude that the
world is uncreated.

ENTROPY. *Energy*, whether potential or kinetic,
is the capacity for doing work. *Work* consists in
changing, against resistance, a body's motion or
position, or its chemical or physical constitution.
Energy has many forms, as that of a mass in motion, heat, light, electricity, the energy of chemical
combination, of mechanical strain, etc. It is an ac-

cepted conclusion from scientific induction that the *amount* of energy in the universe is fixed and invariable; this is called the *conservation of energy*. But amount, or quantity, is here understood to mean the sum total of energy, both available and unavailable. It must be noted, however, that in every transformation of energy, wherever an energizing condition exists, whenever work is done, a certain amount of available energy is lost in diffused heat. Hence, as the useless energy increases, the useful decreases by the same amount. This ratio of useless to useful energy is called *entropy*. The law of entropy states that the ratio is constantly increasing. This means that the amount of energy available for the energizing processes of the world is ever growing less.

Thesis 4. The present state of the material world, in so far as the conditions necessary for life are concerned, will eventually come to an end

Argument. The available energy in the world is continually decreasing. But such decrease means the ultimate cessation of conditions requisite for life. Therefore the conditions requisite for life will eventually come to an end.

The major. A certain amount of the energy at work is always converted into heat. Now heat is indeed a form of energy, but it is not available unless it can flow into a body of lower temperature. The result of this operation is that all the bodies in the universe will gradually approach the same temperature. Hence the amount of available energy is constantly approaching zero.

The minor. We know that organisms cannot

subsist except under conditions where considerable energy is available; in fact they are able to subsist on earth only by virtue of the energy which has been and is being constantly diffused in space by the heavenly bodies. Plant-life is possible only by the utilization of energy radiated from the sun. Plants in turn supply food and oxygen for the animal kingdom. Thus the whole of organic life is dependent on a constant and enormous flow of energy.

Difficulties. 1. Available energy can be restored by collisions among the stars.

Reply. The heat generated by a collision constitutes a decided loss in the colliding bodies; and although the rest of the universe might profit for a while by the increase of heat, the entropy in the universe as a whole is considerably hastened by the collision. Thus the earth's life might be prolonged at the expense of the rest of the universe, but death must eventually come even to the most favored spot. Moreover entropy is galloping to its goal at too rapid a rate to be notably checked by the extremely rare collisions of stars.

2. On the supposition that the world is infinite in extent its energy could never be exhausted.

Reply. Those who make that supposition also suppose that the world is of infinite duration; but anything approaching a limit for an infinite period has already reached its goal. Moreover they suppose that what is happening in the rest of the universe is the same as what is happening in the portion we know. But in this portion energy is tending to a uniform distribution of heat within finite time; therefore the same should be true of the entire universe. Finally the expression, "a world of actually infinite extent," is a congeries of words for which no justification can be found either in fact or in concept.

3. The equalization of temperature is an asymptote; but

an asymptote is never reached; therefore the equalization of temperature will never be reached.

Reply. I distinguish the major: the absolutely perfect equalization is such, I grant. The nearly perfect equalization is such, I deny. I concede the minor. I distinguish the conclusion: absolutely perfect equalization will never be reached, I grant: nearly perfect, I deny. It is to be noted that we do not contend that absolute equilibrium will ever be established, even though it is constantly being approached. But we do say that a point will be reached at which world processes which we describe as "the present state of the world" can no longer be carried on.

4. The organisms themselves can convert entropy to "ectropy."

Reply. Organisms are not exempt from the laws of energy. Even when the human will directs the spending of bodily energy, it does just that—directs, does not create it. Besides, the little energy which organisms could be supposed to restore, could never serve so to check the advance of entropy as to stave off their own doom.

5. W. Nernst propounds the hypothesis that the stars by expending their own substance through the ether are building up other stars elsewhere which will repeat the process. Therefore the world is not running down.

Reply. This man, who has done some good work in science, reflects little credit on himself by that hypothesis. As a matter of fact his argument is upside-down. He begins with the premise that the world is not running down, and concludes that therefore there must be some process by which its energy is restored. That way of proceeding is serviceable in an attempt to discover evidence; but it is wrong, without having discovered the evidence, to reverse the order of the propositions and present them as a proof. And even his suggestions, as to "how it might be done," are contrary to all observed facts. We cannot demand evidence in science, and abandon it when we philosophize.

6. Clerk Maxwell postulated a "demon" to restore the energy.

Reply. That is mere humor. Even if taken seriously it substantiates our thesis that nature cannot do it by itself.

The Beginning of the World in Time

The Scholastics in the Middle Ages discussed whether an eternal world were possible, and generally held that it was not. St. Thomas, as is well known, maintained that the impossibility of such a world could not be demonstrated; and until such demonstration were forthcoming he feared it should be an uncalled-for affront to his Arabian adversaries to assert that their thesis was intrinsically absurd. Eternity as applied to a world was not understood to be the same kind as the eternity of God. God's eternity has no succession; whereas world-duration is clearly one of succession. By "eternal world" the Scholastics meant a world without a beginning in time. And their query was totally apart from the question of creation. To ask whether the world had a beginning in time is not identical with asking whether it is created. For, even supposing such a world to exist, that fact would not exclude the need of its being created. Creation does not directly refer to the duration of the world, but to the reason for its existence; and it means that the reason for the world's existence is not within itself but in Another. Creation means that the world is *ab alio*. Granted an omnipotent God, then He can produce anything that is not a contradiction. Therefore, if an "eternal" world is not a contradiction, God could produce such a world. The point of the dispute is whether the phrase "eternal world," or "world without a beginning," contains an intrinsic contradiction. Some modern writers, who, without any warrant, accept the phrase as expressing the fact about the present world and then from that assumption jump to the conclusion that the world is uncreated, are too much bent on their objective to care for logic.

St. Thomas was a neutral in the discussion, withholding his assent until he should have proof. For all that, an "eternal" world seems to be a contradiction. For, supposing such a world, then, at the present moment the number of events is, not merely indefinitely large, but actually infinite; and that number is increased in the next moment. The same is true not only of the present moment, but of any moment whatsoever in the past. If you remember that we are not dealing with the "infinite" of mathematics, but with actually existing beings, the supposition cannot be defended from the charge of intrinsic inconsistency.

Aristotle maintained that God introduced order into the world, and this constituted the beginning of the cosmos, as it did of time. From the succession and finality of the world he argued to a supramundane Cause and Prime Mover; but it must be admitted that he did not grasp production without a material cause, and consequently groped blindly for an explanation of the origin of matter. This failure ultimately to distinguish between Creator and creature as such, was a result of his overconcentration on his reply to the Atomists, and Eleatics. Against them he demonstrated the reality of change, but in so doing overlooked the possibility of change improperly so called, viz., creation.[2]

Topics for Discussion. The conservation of energy. The dissipation of energy. "Energy pumps." Why are perpetual motion machines impossible? The probability of the collision of the solar system with other systems, with clouds of meteors. The result of the retardation of planetary motion. Tides as a retardation of the revolution of the earth, as of the moon. Possibility of the earth's losing its atmosphere. St. Thomas' monograph *De aeternitate mundi.* How old is the earth? the universe?

REFERENCES

Cath. Ency. "The Universe," Part 2.

Duff, A. *Text-Book of Physics,* p. 291.

Husslein, J. *Evolution and Social Progress,* Ch. 10.

Joly, J. *Birthtime of the World.*

Maxwell, J. Clerk. *Theory of Heat,* "On Entropy," p. 162.

Scient. Amer. Monthly, Vol. 135, p. 72. "Creation."

Stallo, J. *Concepts and Theories of Modern Physics.*

Webster, Farwell and Drew. *General Physics for Colleges,* p. 226.

[2] Cf. *Phys.* I. 8.

CHAPTER V

MONISM

DEFINITIONS. Monism is any philosophical tenet the import of which is that there exists and can exist only one entity, one being, independent, unrelated to any other, self-sufficient, the sole constituent principle of all apparently different beings and identical in fact with them all. Monism is therefore the name used to designate all those philosophical schools which are represented by such aphorisms as the following: "All is Brahma" (Hindu Phil.); "There is only one substance" (Spinoza); "The Ego posits itself" (Fichte); "The individual is the universal" (Hegel); "Nothing is except matter" (Haeckel); "God is the infinite world with its nisus towards deity" (S. Alexander).[1] In the conception last indicated, "deity" does not exist, and never shall; for it is always the next remove ahead in the world's evolution. *Pantheism* begins with God and identifies the world with Him. *Materialism* begins with matter and identifies mind and God with matter. Both kinds of Monism hold that there is an "Absolute" whose "parts," "modes," "forms," "modifications," "manifestations," etc., make up the world. Monism is opposed to *Pluralism,* which holds that there are many substances,

[1] Cf. *Space, Time and Deity,* Vol. 2, p. 353.

and to *Dualism,* which classifies substances as God and creature, spirit and matter, living and non-living.

HISTORY OF MONISM. *Brahmanism,* originating about the fourteenth century B.C., teaches that "what is, is Brahma; what is not Brahma is nothing," that Brahma is both the efficient and the material cause of the world, that he is the being of all things. The *Eleatics,* beginning with the abstract notion of being, as such, identified the real order with the ideal, denied multiplicity and change, and the reliability of the senses; they, however, descended sufficiently from the abstract notion of being to include life, and so professed hylozoistic Monism, or Panpsychism. The *Stoics,* maintaining that all things, spirit, soul and God were corporeal, and that all men were parts of a universal being, were in the final analysis, materialistic Monists, Determinists and Fatalists. The *Neoplatonists* and *Gnostics* taught that from God everything else emanated, without being entirely distinct from Him. In the Middle Ages *Scotus Erigena* and *Eckhart* professed a kind of Pantheism, derived from the Neoplatonists. *Spinoza,* the high priest of modern Pantheism, began with the ambiguous definition of substance given by Descartes, to the effect that a substance is that which needs no other being. Substance does not indeed need a subject in which to exist. Descartes' definition, taken simply as it stands, designates not merely substance, *ens per se,* but God, *Ens a Se.* It was this last meaning that Spinoza chose; hence to him every substance was divine, and divine substance is only one. To this substance Spinoza ascribes two "attributes," thought and extension; "particular things" being merely modes of expression for these attributes. Modern Monists usually designate the one entity by the word "Absolute." Thus for *Paulsen* the Absolute evolves through a succession of coherent modification. For *Hegel*

the Absolute is neither spiritual nor material, but something apart from both these orders, and evolves by dialectic, or logical, necessity. *Schopenhauer,* in his revolt from Hegelianism, makes the Absolute a will instead of an idea, and a will that is doomed to utter disappointment. The *Materialist,* as *Haeckel,* is a Monist, only in the sense that he admits but one kind of being, namely matter. There is not here one individual. Still the fashion is to refer to nature as an Absolute and one being, as is done by Alexander in the quotation cited above. An outline of this man's doctrine will serve as an example of present day teaching. According to Professor Alexander, the stuff from which all things are made is space-time. Space-time is motion in itself without the motion of a body; time is its soul; space its body. From space-time springs, by evolution, matter. Now matter is the soul of time, the latter serving as body. Matter in turn becomes body for a further soul, life. Life then becomes a body for mind. That is as far as we have gotten. The next evolution is "Deity," so called because it is the unattainable morrow. When our morrow becomes to-day, it will be "a finite God or angel"; and "Deity" will still be the morrow. Once, too, we were matter, but were swept on "by that restless movement of time which is not the mere turning of a squirrel in its cage, but the nisus toward a higher birth." [2]

THEOSOPHY. Theosophy is rather a *method* than a doctrine. Just as rational philosophy seeks to know God by a study of His creatures, and as theology seeks a knowledge of Him, and especially of His free decrees, by a study of His direct teaching, so theosophy makes the claim to know Him by direct intuition of His essence. Now the obvious objects of our cognition are what we call "crea-

[2] Cf. *Space, Time and Deity,* Vol. 2, p. 348ff.

tures." To avoid this difficulty theosophy postulates that the divine essence is immanent in all creatures, inherent in them. They profess to see the One in the all, and the all in the One. Their postulate, or supposition, is clearly pantheistic. In this, theosophy is widely different from Christian mysticism, which always intellectually distinguishes God from creatures, and uses the latter to impel the will toward *another* Object, namely the extramundane personal Creator.

DIVISIONS OF MONISM. Monism strictly so called is Pantheism, which maintains that everything is one *individual;* less strictly it is Materialism, or Naturalism, which holds that everything is one *kind* of being, viz., matter. *Ideal* Pantheism asserts the existence of the ego alone, with everything else as empty apparitions; *Real* Pantheism admits the reality of the objects of our cognition.

Thesis 5. Pantheism and materialistic Monism contradict both reason and experience

Part I. Pantheism

Argument. Reason and experience demonstrate nothing more clearly than the plurality of beings; but Pantheism denies the plurality of beings; therefore Pantheism contradicts both reason and experience.

The major. 1. Each of us is *conscious* that he is distinct from the world about him. A prisoner in a cell is aware that he is not imposing confinement on himself. A pugilist in the ring cannot think that his opponent is none other than himself, and that it is exactly the same thing to receive a blow as to deliver one. To shave one's self is a different thing from having the barber do it. When the dentist pulls my tooth, I know that the patient and the agent are not one. When a rough sea tosses me about, I am quite sure there is something besides myself in existence. Moreover, some actions are to my knowledge decidedly my own; as for instance when I hold my breath. If I cannot know these things, there is nothing I can know.

2. The world revealed to me by my *external senses* is clearly made up of a plurality of things. Man has intelligence; brutes have life without intelligence; plants have life without sensation; the rest of the material world has no life at all. Who can tell me that all these things are one, without asking me to abandon reason? If all these things are one, then it is as true to say that the grass ate the horse, as that the horse ate the grass: in either case the one ate itself. And if, in compliance with the Idealistic Pantheists, I reject all knowledge of the external world, then with equal right I reject all knowledge of consciousness, and I have no knowledge left.

3. If all the facts of internal and external experience do not constitute reasonable evidence of plurality, what may I claim as bona fide evidence that things are all one? If I cannot know what I am distinct from the world, or that the world is made up of distinct things, surely I cannot be expected to know that space-time is the ultimate entity, that it is motion without anything moving, that there

is an event-particle half way between space and time, nor the rest of the claptrap that goes with the various theories of Monism.

The minor. That is the one proposition on which all Pantheists agree. And the only one.

Part II. Materialistic Monism

Argument. There is an essential difference between the living and non-living, between sense and intellect, as is shown in psychology; but where there is merely one kind of being, i.e., matter, with the same forces everywhere, there cannot be essential differences: Therefore there is no solitary reality, such as mere matter.

The major, besides being obvious, is formally demonstrated in psychology, and is in accord with unprejudiced scientific experiment. To quote but one scientist:

> The conception of the universe as nothing but a set of one or a few kinds of particles moving according to a few immutable laws exemplified at any time and anywhere that particles occur, is pitiful in its inadequacy. . . . The method of science based on this motion is a false one. . . . New things and new modes of action distinguish the living from the non-living, the sentient from the non-sentient, the reasoning from the non-reasoning.

And after showing that organisms are essentially diverse from inorganic matter, and from one another, he continues:

No longer can the biologist be bullied into suppressing observed results because they are not discovered nor expected from work on the non-living parts of nature.

Again:

No ground based on experimental analysis can be alleged for the assertion that the mental does not affect the physical; this is a purely a priori notion. . . . Thought, purpose, ideals, conscience, do alter what happens. . . . A particular individual . . . may act in ways that are diverse from those of any other individual under the same outer circumstances. . . . The statement that the laws of nature are immutable must not be construed to mean that new laws shall not be exemplified.[3]

The minor. The Materialist maintains that there is nothing but matter in existence, that matter is the only reality; that there is no activity except physical and chemical reactions, the so-called mechanical interplay of forces in space; that these material forces are everything that is—life, consciousness, reason, God. Most writers of this school at the present day decline the name "Materialist," and prefer "Naturalist," but the doctrine has not changed with the name.

Parts I and II (together)

Argument. An Absolute Being identical with the world is repugnant to reason and experience; but Monism supposes such a being; therefore . . .

[3] H. S. Jennings, *Science*, Jan. 14, 1927.

The major. Such a being, as is demonstrated in theodicy, is infinite and immutable. But all forms of Monism admit a changing, and hence a finite world. The same is clearly evident to our experience. Therefore the world cannot be identical with the Absolute, or Necessary Being.

The minor. Monism teaches that the Absolute is the sole reality.

Note. It is clear that Monism is destructive of religion, since religion is based on the recognition of a distinct, personal, supramundane God. The Monist's admission of "religion" as a sentiment is a misuse of the term. The direct tendency of Monism is toward the glorification of self, and to absolutism or despotism in government. It also destroys morality by removing legislator, liberty and sanction. Every license is justified as the natural expression of self, and inevitable.

Difficulties. 1. The Infinite includes everything; therefore there can be nothing apart from the Infinite.

Reply. I distinguish the antecedent: the Infinite includes all perfections, I grant; the Infinite includes all beings, I deny. I distinguish the consequent likewise: there cannot be any perfection anywhere distinct from the Infinite, without there being a counterpart of that perfection in the Infinite, I grant; there cannot be any being distinct from the Infinite, I deny. The idea of an Infinite Being does not exclude other beings; it signifies that no other being can possess a perfection which the Infinite Being does not possess. It may be noted, too, that finite beings possess their perfections mixed with imperfections, even if the imperfections be nothing more than the very limitations of nature. Thus an apple may be perfect but is still subject to the limitations of its species. This is what we mean by mixed perfections. In the Infinite Being there are only unmixed perfections. Some perfections of finite beings include *in their very notion* an imperfection, e.g., extension. A body is present in various parts of space, but only part by part; where one part is present the rest is absent. The Infinite Being is entirely present in any part, and that too without being absent from the others. In this way God does not possess extension as such, or formally, because extension in its very notion implies an imperfection; He possesses such perfections eminently and virtually; that is to say, the corresponding perfection in God is of a higher order, implying no imperfection; in this case it is His immensity, or His omnipresence. Other perfections of finite beings, as life, intellect, do not in their very concept imply an imperfection; these perfections God possesses *both eminently and formally;* eminently because intellect in God is infinite, whereas in the creature it is *de facto* finite; formally because intellect as such is possessed by both, and is directly predicated of each. Thus we see that the Infinite Being always possesses the counterpart of finite perfections, and always in a higher, that is to say, in the infinite order. It is clear from this that an increase in the number of beings does not in any way increase the sum of extant perfection.

2. The mind seeks to reduce all to a unity; but this is what is done by Monism.

Reply. The mind does seek to reduce all changeable things to a unity of origin as their first cause, and by a continual broadening of general concepts to come at last to the all embracing concept of being as such; but the mind cannot without contradiction assert the identity of changing things with the necessarily changeless First Cause, nor affirm the actual existence of universals as such, much less the existence of transcendental being as such. To arrive at such a reduction would moreover contradict the premises which supposed there was something to reduce.

3. The Infinite Being is existence itself—*ipsum esse,* and therefore is identical with every existent.

Reply. The Infinite Being is called "existence itself" because He exists necessarily, so that His non-existence is utterly impossible; but that does not mean that He is identical with contingent beings. Quite the contrary.

4. God is in all things.

Reply. He is the efficient cause and exemplary cause of all other things, and is present to them, I grant; He is a constituent of all things, I deny.

5. "The universal harmony of all things is intelligible only if we admit that they are all members of one being, one substance" (Paulsen).

Reply. That harmony is intelligible on the principle that the separate beings were so designed and collocated as to produce the harmony; and without such designing and juxtaposition even the various parts of one substance could not result in harmony. Nor do the parts of a machine have to be all one piece in order to coöperate harmoniously. More than that, human beings, in matters where each as a free agent is a law unto himself, may combine their activities harmoniously, as in a drill or an orchestra performance, without at the same time becoming physically one individual.

Topics for Discussion. The Stoic doctrine of a world soul. The relation of Pantheism to Fatalism. The doctrine of immanence. Theosophy. Change inexplicable in the monistic doctrine.

REFERENCES

Balmes, J. *Fundamental Philosophy,* Vol. 2.
Cath. Ency. "Immanence." "Monism" (in "Cosmology").
    "Mind and Matter." "Pantheism." "Materialism."

Cath. World, Vol. 27, p. 471. "Atheism vs. Pantheism."
Devas, C. *Key to the World's Progress,* p. 31.
Hull, E. *Theosophy and Christianity.*
Lord, D. *Armchair Philosophy.*
Martindale, C. *Theosophy.*
Month, Vol. 109, p. 600. "The Higher Pantheism."
Ryan, J. H. *An Introduction to Philosophy,* Ch. 2.
Wasmann, E. *Christian Monism.*

PART II

THE COMMON PROPERTIES OF BODIES

SECTION 1. EXTENSION, OR INTEGRAL COMPOSITION

CHAPTER VI

THE NATURE OF EXTENSION

THE NOTION OF EXTENSION. Extension is that property of all bodies which we describe by saying that they have parts outside of parts. It is a property which is involved in all our sense perceptions, since the senses cannot perceive bodies unless they are extended. Being thus a content of sense impression, it cannot be defined by essential definition, giving true genus and specific difference. Even a *descriptive definition,* like the one above, cannot avoid using terms that involve the very thing to be defined. In the definition given, the words "parts" and "outside," in the sense in which they are understood there, imply the notion of extension. The same fate awaits a genetic definition. I may, for instance, say that extension is generated by a moving point, or by a line moving transversely, or a plane moved in the same manner. But here motion and direction involve the notion of space. However, since extension is a matter of universal sense experience, there is no need to define it accurately. It is enough to point out what we mean by the word. And by "extension" in the thesis we mean any or all of the three dimensions.

ARISTOTLE ON QUANTITY. Aristotle's definition of extension, or quantity, is famous. He says: "Quantity is that which is divisible into components, each of which qualifies as a single and complete entity."[1] It must be admitted that Aristotle here defines quantity in the concrete; that is, he defines an extended body. Besides, the definition is consciously descriptive, since it starts with the property of divisibility. Still it is well for our purpose to note the points he chooses for his description: (1) Extension is *divisible,* therefore *undivided;* (2) after division, each resultant quantity is *one,* single, undivided, as was the original; (3) each resultant is complete, therefore *not* a *part,* it can be considered by itself as something entire in itself. Thus, when you divide a line in two; each of the two qualifies as a line as truly as did the original one; and each of the two is a complete unity in itself. In a word, the things which you predicate of the original quantity, you can predicate in exactly the same sense of the resultants of your division. Division affects the relative size of the resulting extensions, but does not in any way affect the true nature of extension; each of the resultants is as truly *one, complete* and *divisible* as the quantity that suffered division.

CONTINUOUS AND DISCONTINUOUS EXTENSION. *Continuous* extension is *uninterrupted* extension, an unbroken stretch or expanse; it may be a line, a plane or a solid. The moment any of these is severed in two, by a point, line or plane, it has ceased to be continuous, and is then called *discrete.* By discrete we therefore mean quantity which is *discontinuous.* Discrete quantity is twofold: it is *contiguous* if the two or more quantities are in contact; it is *separate* if there is an interval between them.

[1] *Metaph.* IV. 13.

Thus, to use a homely illustration, a single brick may represent continuous extension, two bricks in contact contiguous extension, two bricks with mortar between them separate extension. It should be noted that only continuous quantity is a unit; discrete quantity is a *group* of units.

THE MYSTERY OF THE CONTINUUM. In the present thesis we have to deal with extension only. It is not pertinent here to raise the question: Are bodies, such as a brick, really continuous? We have as a matter of fact a clear notion of continuous extension, and we constantly deal with such extension in geometry. We know what we mean by an unbroken line, an unbroken plane, an unbroken solid. Whether bodies which we see, as a sheet of paper, are actually continuous in their visible matter, does not concern us here. Whatever suggests the notion of continuous extension, it is certainly a notion common to us all. The thesis, when limited in this way, scarcely has any adversaries; though many, as Leibnitz and Balmes, confess that the inexhaustible divisibility of a continuum is a profound mystery. The mystery may be exemplified in the following diagram.

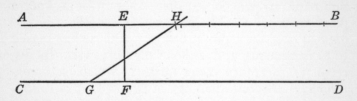

AB is parallel to CD, and EF perpendicular to them. The line GH is pivoted at G, and is swung

to different positions along AB. In each swing
outward toward B, another portion is cut off EF.
But however far I carry the point H along the pro-
longation of AB, I can never exhaust my division of
EF. This mystery, however, is a thing most common in mathematics, and is dealt with in the theory
of limits.

QUANTITY NOT REDUCED. The comprehension
of that mystery is, happily, not necessary to an
understanding of the thesis. The simple fact which
we have to consider is this: when I divide a line
(or plane or solid), I have as much line (or plane
or solid) left after the division as I had before.
The sum of the quantity is not being reduced in the
slightest degree by my divisions and hence is *not
even approaching* a limit. The "mystery" does not
concern the quantity as such but only the number
and size of the sections.

WHAT "CONTINUUM" SIGNIFIES. The first part
of the thesis may be stated thus: a line is not made
up of points, a plane is not made up of lines, a
volume is not made up of planes. The proposition
is scarcely more than a mathematical one, and is
almost too obvious to need proof; but on account
of its intimate connection with the nature of matter,
extension must be clearly understood. The proof,
then, need not be more than expository of *the true
character of extension*. Some terms, moreover, in
the second part of the thesis should be correctly
understood. The term *"mathematical division"* is
employed because division reduces the size of the
resulting quantities, which may thus become too
small to permit physical division by any instruments

at our command. We grant, therefore, that we may proceed with actual cutting or severing of an extended body down to a certain limit beyond which we are unable to pass for the sheer lack of means by which to continue the division. Thus, at the present day we have been able to divide bodies into atoms, and atoms into electrons and nuclei. Further than that we are as yet unable to go. These particles remain for us *physically indivisible*. But they are mathematically divisible, for they have extension. Mathematical division is not hindered by the minuteness of the body, nor by its inward construction. The only thing mathematically indivisible is a mathematical point. A point has no extension; it is the negation of extension. But where there is *extension* there is *divisibility*, for the terms are convertible in the sense in which they are used here. Briefly, then, we assert that whatever may impede our division, it is not the lack of extension in the sections still to be divided. Each of these sections is a *continuum* as truly as the original, and presents the same inexhaustible divisibility as any other.

To Illustrate the Point at Issue. In order to put this fact in a clearer light, it may be helpful to imagine that I have something before me which I intend to divide. Let us say a yard-measure. I am provided with a knife so sharp that it does not crush the wood in any way, nor carry any of the substance away with it in the process. Now I will suppose that I cut the yard-measure exactly in the middle; and at the moment I do so, I myself shrink to one-half my former size. I then see that the half-yard presents the same problem to me as did the yard; and when I sever the half-yard, I shrink as before. By this illustration we eliminate the difficulty about the size of the object to be divided, and can see that any components to which we may reduce a given extension are themselves extended, and as truly divisible as the original quantity.

DIVISIBILITY. The term "indefinitely divisible" signifies that division may always proceed beyond any of the definite stages at which division has actually stopped, and beyond any number of divisions, however many, which you may choose to designate. The term, nevertheless, does not imply that there is any such thing as an actually infinite number. The *actual division* is always definite in number, and finite; the *capability of division* is never exhausted by any number of actual divisions, but *always remains*. The number of divisions is *"potentially infinite,"* but never actually infinite. As we have seen, divisions of a continuum result in other continua. Since the *essence* of a continuum is to be *undivided and divisible,* division only multiplies the continua, without affecting the essence of any of them.

Thesis 6. Continuous extension is not made up of indivisible components; hence it is indefinitely capable of mathematical division

Part I

Argument. In the matter of extension, the only indivisibles are mathematical points; but continuous extension is not made up of these; therefore continuous extension is not made up of indivisible components.

The minor. If the points are separated they do not form a continuum. If they are in contact they all coalesce into one point, and hence do not form any extension whatever.

Part II

Argument. If continuous extension is *not* capable of indefinite mathematical division, then there must be ultimate parts beyond which division cannot conceivably proceed; but there can be no such ultimate parts: therefore continuous extension is indefinitely capable of mathematical division.

The major. To arrive at ultimate parts is the only way divisibility could come to an end.

The minor. The ultimate parts must be either extended or inextended. If extended, they are still divisible, and hence not *ultimate*. If inextended, they are *not parts;* for points are zero extension (not merely infinitesimally small extension), and no sum of them could ever constitute any extension.

The Parts of a Continuum

The thesis we have established denied that a continuum can have ultimate parts. The next question raised is: Can a continuum have *any* parts? At first thought it would seem that it cannot have; for, although divisible, it is essentially single and undivided. If we actually divide it, the result is two or more continua, each of which is again an undivided unit. A continuum is not a thing of parts, it is all "one part." And still it is *divisible,* which fact seems to imply parts. The philosophical answer is that a continuum is *actually one and potentially many*.

In order to understand the meaning of this answer, let us first consider a process which is the reverse of division. A mechanic, let us say, has a number of bars of iron, and we will suppose for the sake of argument that they are continuous. Each bar is a unit in itself. The mechanic considers welding two of them into one piece. The moment he entertains the idea the contemplated result assumes in his mind the nature of a unit or total, and the two bars drop to the rank of parts or halves. If he considers welding three bars together, they become thirds of the one resultant bar. Thus the bars are actually many but potentially one; and their rank as parts depends on the total contemplated by the mind.

The converse of this is true, if, instead of welding, the mechanic considers cutting one of the bars into sections. The bar is actually one piece. It is an integer. There are in it no fractions *as such* until they are assigned by the mind. The truth of this last statement will become clear by considering that if the mechanic intends to divide the bar in halves, a certain division is projected; if into thirds, another division is projected which negatives the first. The two are incompatible simultaneously. And not only do the fractions thus overlap, but the number of pieces into which a continuum is divisible is potentially infinite: to say that the parts are actually there before being assigned is the same as affirming an actually infinite number in every part of space great and small, and that moreover all the finite divisions exist simultaneously with the infinite ones. We repeat, then, that before parts are assigned there is actually only one integer, and no definite fractions whatever. The integer, nevertheless, is a *real foundation* for any fractions that may be assigned. Over the actual integer before him the mechanic superimposes a prospective division. He may draw a mark on the bar to indicate the projected division, and he can say with objective truth that the bar is made up of these definite parts. He then divides it at the line marked. The division does not produce any new iron, it merely severs what was there. After the actual division he may refer to the segments as "parts" only in reference to the total they once formed. But the segments are themselves actual integers now, and like every continuum are undivided units.

A continuum, therefore, has no parts, except indefinitely, fundamentally and potentially—until definite parts are assigned, and then these definite parts can be said to be there as such, or "formally." Thus every continuum is actually one and potentially many.

Difficulties. 1. Continuous extension supposes that there are no internal boundaries in a line, a plane or a volume; but to suppose that there is no boundary or terminus between, e.g., the right half and the left half is absurd; therefore continuous extension is absurd.

Reply. Continuous extension supposes that there are no internal boundaries actually, I grant. It supposes that there is not even a potential boundary or terminus at a given point, I deny. The designation of such terminus is extrinsic to the continuum, namely, in the mind. We may even designate the potential terminus by a mark, as is done in geometry by a dotted line, without considering that we have severed the continuous extension.

2. Then, the parts have no limits until I designate them. But what has no limits is infinite in extent.

Reply. All the parts that can be designated lie within the actual outer limits of the whole continuum, and hence it is folly to pretend that any of them could be infinite in extent.

3. But the parts are infinite in number.

Reply. There are no parts until designated. If we could ever succeed in designating an infinite number, there would be that many parts; but not otherwise.

4. A perfect sphere touches a plane in only one point, and if the sphere be rolled along the plane its path is a line. Now, that line cannot be formed except by the addition of points; but what is formed by the addition of points is composed of points; therefore a continuum may be made up of indivisible components.

Reply. First of all, when the sphere is standing still the fact of contact indicates one point in the plane and one in the surface of the sphere; the moment the sphere rolls those two points separate. To speak of the point of contact with the rolling sphere is to employ a figure of speech, for any given point either in the sphere or the plane instantly ceases to be the point of contact. If, however, the objector chose to drag his sphere over the plane instead of rolling it, he would have had at least one point of contact which remained constant, namely the one on the surface of the sphere. He is then drawing a line with a rather clumsy pencil. But even in this case his argument is not valid. We grant that when the pencil is stationary its point is in contact with one point in the plane. But the moving point of the pencil can never be coincident with any given point in the plane. For, if it move, how-

ever briefly, it is describing a line; and a line cannot be
coincident with a point. Only by zero movement can the
point on the pencil be made coincident with any given
point in the plane; but zero movement means a full stop.
Thus we deny the supposition of the major—the supposition, viz., that a moving point can be coincident with a
stationary one.

5. Achilles pursuing Hector runs twice as fast as the
latter, but never overtakes him. Let us suppose that they
are a hundred yards apart at the start. When Achilles
covers the hundred yards, Hector is fifty yards in front.
When Achilles covers the fifty, Hector is twenty-five in
advance, then twelve and a half, and so on without end.

Reply. The objection labors under the same false supposition as the previous one, to wit, that a moving point
can be coincident with a stationary one. The point of
Achilles' spear passes over the point on the ground which
marks the end of the hundred yards, but it is never *at* that
point for any instant of time however brief. To be at it,
or coincident with it, the point of the spear should have
to be brought to a complete stop. And if it had to make a
complete stop at the end of each diminishing distance, as
indicated, it could of course never reach the back of the
fleeing Hector. Zeno, from whom the objection is taken,
(though he illustrates with a tortoise instead of Hector)
strives, like other captious dialecticians down to our own
day, to fool himself and his readers with such conundrums
in order to have an excuse for skepticism. Happily, in
default of any other answer, we can generally use the
probatur ambulando against these sophistries.

Topics for Discussion. Palmieri's "points." The
theory of Boscovich. Quantity in extension and in
number. Genetic definitions of lines, planes and
solids. Is the motion of the pendulum continuous

or discrete: that is, does the pendulum come to rest at the end of each swing, or on the contrary can it be truly said that there is no interval of time however brief during which the pendulum is motionless?

REFERENCES

Cath. Ency. "Extension." "Quantity." "Infinity." "Boscovich."

O'Neill, J. *Cosmology,* Vol. 1, Ch. 7.

CHAPTER VII

THE FACT OF EXTENSION

THE DIVISIBILITY OF BODIES. We have seen that continuous extension in the abstract is inexhaustibly divisible. In other words it is always divisible into divisible sections, but never into indivisible ones. The question which now faces us is whether there is any such extension in the concrete, whether existing bodies are divisible down to certain final indivisible components. We answer that they are not. We affirm that no matter how far actual division may have progressed the resulting particles are still divisible. As a matter of fact, actual division in our day has resulted in isolating *electrons* and certain *nuclei*. Scientists for the present are content that the electron is "indivisible," and they feel that if they can succeed in separating out a single *proton* they shall have arrived at another "indivisible." But what they mean by "indivisible" is something which they have no means, and can foresee no means, of dividing. These particles of matter are indivisible *to us;* they are not indivisible *in themselves;* they are not mathematical points. Science gives their diameter, which, though very small, is an extent, and therefore not a point. They may be *extrinsically* indivisible, but *not intrin-*

sically so. If they are extended at all they are intrinsically divisible. What we assert in the thesis is that a body cannot be reduced by division to inextended components.

EVERY PARTICLE OF MATTER HAS SOME EXTENSION. Another consideration which may give us pause is the following. It is possible, or at least conjecturable, that matter simply cannot exist in infinitesimally thin slices. If, for instance, I were able, by means as yet unknown, to slice up a proton into millions of laminae, and then repeat the process on one of the pieces, I might conceivably reach a point at which matter would no longer stand up under the process, and at that point would defy all the efficiency of the universe to divide it further. We propose this conjecture, not as anything about which we wish to take sides, but to clear up the state of the question in this thesis. Then, at that last stand of matter against further division, the particle of matter making the stand would be indivisible, and that *for intrinsic reasons.* We grant that, in the supposition made, the reasons are intrinsic, but we maintain that there is one intrinsic reason which is not a bar to further division, and that is the *fact of extension* in the particle making the last stand. The impossibility of further division is not due to the lack of extension. The particle is not a point, nor a mathematical plane.

TWO KINDS OF CONTINUA. Continuous extension as applied to bodies is three dimensional. But it must be noted here that such extension is of two kinds; namely, that which is continuous *along all lines,* and that which is continuous *along certain lines only.* In the first kind a line connecting any two points in the body will lie entirely within the body. Thus a cube is continuous along all lines, as is also a sphere. In the second kind a line connecting certain pairs of points will not lie wholly within the body. A ring, for example, is continuous along certain lines; but a straight line joining opposite ends of the diameter will not lie wholly within the ring, it will pass out into the open space and reënter the ring at the other side. So, too, a crescent-shaped body is not continuous along all lines, nor a body shaped like a net, or sponge, or shell, etc. Still such bodies are *truly continuous;* for you can, so to speak, go from any point in the body to any other, without going outside it, provided you follow certain lines. So long as the body is continuous along some line or other it is a continuum. If there is no line of continuity the quantity is not continuous but discrete. Hence our thesis does not concern the *shape* of the matter which it asserts to be continuous; nor does it deny that there may be complete vacua, totally empty space, within the compass of a continuous body—since the body may be in the shape of a cylinder, a link in a chain, a hollow sphere, a sponge, or any sort of porous construction. When, therefore, we say that a body is continuous we do not necessarily mean that the whole body is *absolutely solid.*

Two Kinds of Matter. The next point to be made clear is: Of what bodies do we pretend to speak? In answer it is to be noticed that the wording of the thesis does not specify any bodies in particular, it merely mentions "portions of matter."

Under the term "portions" we wish to include even particles too minute to be directly visible by any means in our power; and under the term "matter" we include *imponderable* matter as well as *ponderable matter*. The ether (granting that it exists) is matter, for it is extended substance; and although it is insensible matter, its existence and properties are known from their sensible results. The extent of imponderable matter is greater than that of ponderable matter, even within the compass of visible bodies. We say that matter is continuous somewhere; about the number and size of the continuous portions we do not propose to offer any verdict.

SCOPE OF THE THESIS. Criteriology establishes the *objective reality* of the extended world. It is not our purpose to reëstablish it here. We take it as proved and patent that extension is the basis of all sense perception, that vision and feeling report extension as an attribute of every object they take in, that the sense organs and their activities are all extended, that motion which is so universal in the world is unintelligible without an extended field. Nor are we concerned with the *genesis* of our perception of relative size and distance; that is a subject for experimental psychology. It is the province of cosmology to accept the fact of extension as a datum, and then to analyze the fact and determine its implications with respect to existing bodies. In the previous thesis we considered the notion of a continuum. We now take a quantity which is admittedly not continuous, namely, the large expanse of matter about us. It is not continuous, for we admit that it is actually divided into segments large and small. We grant that the world is not continuous throughout, that the sum of the extension in the world of our daily experience is discrete extension, that a man is not continuous with the house he lives in, or the machine he drives. The house itself is a sum of discrete parts, and the machine likewise. Familiar portions of the material world are thus evidently made up of discrete components. We do not deny that; what we do deny is that matter is made up of discrete components *in the last analysis*. We maintain that actual division stops somewhere, that there are ultimate portions, whatever their size, which, although they are divisible, mathematically at least, are nevertheless *de facto* undivided. The thesis is so reasonable in itself that the argument need not be much more than expository.

Thesis 7. In the material universe there must be ultimate portions of matter which have continuous extension

Argument. Matter as we experience it in our daily life is a sum of smaller components; but it could not be such a sum unless the ultimate components have continuous extension; therefore in the material universe there must be ultimate portions of matter which have continuous extension.

The major is admitted by all.

The minor. If the *de facto* ultimate components are not continuous, they are without any extension,[1] they are absolute zero extension, and no sum of them could equal extension.

Corollary. As the division of extension cannot

[1] Thesis 6.

end in indivisible units, so the building up of extension cannot begin with indivisible units.

Topics for Discussion. The ultimate particles of matter. The structure of atoms and molecules. The integral composition of bodies. Nuclei, protons and electrons. The quantum theory. Intra-atomic ether. The ether of interstellar space.

REFERENCES

Bragg, W. *Concerning the Nature of Things.*
Cath. Ency. "Extension."
Kramers and Holst. *The Atom and the Bohr Theory of Its Structure.*
Lodge, O. *Atoms and Rays.*
Millikan, A. *The Electron.*

CHAPTER VIII

THE HYPOTHESIS OF INEXTENDED COMPONENTS

REASON FOR DISTINCT THESIS. The dynamist doctrine as stated above is a direct contradiction of Thesis 7. Since we here reject that doctrine we are doing nothing more than reasserting the previous thesis. The whole subject of Dynamism, as restricted here, might have been handled as objections to Thesis 7. Nevertheless it seems better for the sake of clarity and on account of the importance of the subject to give the discussion in a separate thesis.

LIMITATION OF THE THESIS. Dynamism has two meanings: one meaning concerns the *integral composition* of bodies, the other concerns their *essential composition*. It is with the first meaning only that we have to do here. The essential composition of bodies will be taken up later. We are therefore to discuss for the present only the dynamist explanation of *extension*.

THE QUESTION OF SUBSTANCE OR ACCIDENT. Force, as usually understood, is not a substance but an *accident*. Thus the force of the steam in the boiler of an engine is not substance; it is the condition in which the substance water exists there. Owing to the heat and the confinement the water molecules which form the steam are in a state of extreme agitation, so that their combined momentum exerts great pressure on the interior of the boiler and on the cylinder-head. This force is not a substance in itself, but a *state of the substance* water. Still, this force originates in the molecules, and there must therefore be something within the substance itself which makes it act in that way. Hence, though force, as ordinarily understood, is clearly an accident, still the *root-cause of such force must be substance*. If we choose to call this root-cause by the simple name of "force," then force thus understood is a substance. This is what Dynamists actually do; they call force a substance. Rightly understood this statement of theirs may, in the present thesis, be admitted without contention. Even if a Dynamist should speak of forces as if they were accidents and at the same time maintain that they have no connatural subject in which to inhere, he is merely giving the name accident to what is clearly a substance; for an entity which naturally subsists in itself cannot be anything but a substance.

How Space Is Occupied. Aside from Kant, who wonders whether there may really be an extended world about us, the Dynamists in general do not deny that bodies occupy space. Any sizable body, whether it be ocean, pebble or mountain, fills a certain space. In that they agree with us. The disputed point is *how* these bodies fill or occupy the space we concede them. We, on our side, have maintained that the *ultimate integral parts* are extended; the Dynamists say these parts are *inextended*. While Descartes held that the essence of bodies is extension, *Leibnitz* revolted to the opposite extreme and contended that substance, of whatever kind, is nothing but force, or the power of acting, *vis agendi*. "Activity," he says, "is the essence

of substance." Bodies, as a matter of fact, display
the obvious characteristics of force and extension.
We, for our part, accept both as real. We admit
that there is no particle of matter however small
which is totally inert, or without force. On the
other hand we assert in our thesis that these material forces are neither in themselves inextended subjects, or sources, of activity nor do these sources
reside in inextended subjects. The Dynamists assert
that the material world is made up of *point-forces,*
each of which dominates a certain small portion or
volume of empty space, and thus keeps other point-
forces at a distance. They frankly admit action
at a distance, that is *action without any medium
through which* the effect is exerted. Hence, according to them, there is nothing between the ultimate
parts of bodies except empty distance, and the ultimate parts have no extension any more than mathematical points have. This is what they mean by
"occupying" space. Contrariwise, we hold that the
ultimate particles of bodies actually *fill up* the space,
by "being there" so to speak—an assignable part of
the body being in every assignable part of the space
occupied.

HISTORY OF DYNAMISM. In ancient times there are dis-
coverable traces of Dynamism in the writings of Zeno, the
Pythagoreans, and even of Plato. In modern times it first
appears with Giordano Bruno (1600), whose doctrine was
taken up and developed by *Leibnitz* (1716). The latter
calls the ultimate entities "monads," and claims that they
coöperate by reason of "pre-established harmony," that is by
divine prearrangement. Leibnitz's disciple *Wolf* (1754)
exchanged the name of monads for that of "simple entities,"

and discarded all their powers except the mechanical forces of attraction and repulsion. *Boscovich* (1787), a Jesuit mathematician, accepted Wolf's theory, as applied to the inorganic world, and further refined the doctrine of attraction and repulsion. He maintained that the point-elements attracted one another up to a very small distance, but within that small distance they repelled one another. There followed *Balmes* (1848), *Bayma* (1890), and *Carbonelle* (1890). The last named made a distinction between ponderable matter and imponderable, or ether. Both kinds are made up of simple entities, but entities of a like kind repel, while those of opposite kinds attract. To this list may also be added *Lotze, Fechner, Paulsen* and *Hartmann,* who endowed their simple entities with life. Besides the mathematicians already mentioned (Boscovich, Bayma and Carbonelle), we must include such famous scientists as *Ampère* and *Faraday. Palmieri* is the champion of "virtual extension." Perhaps the briefest way to present his doctrine is to say that it is apparently modeled on that of the definitive presence of the soul in the body. Thus the simple entity is represented as being present throughout the sphere of space which it occupies. Palmieri conceives each of these simple entities as having a natural destiny to occupy so much space, and that after the manner of a spirit occupying a body.

CRITICISM OF THE THEORIES. It must be remembered that the various sciences make certain abstractions. If a mathematician is dealing with lines of force emanating from a molecule or an electron, the size of the central particle is so minute as to be *negligible* in certain calculations, and hence he may find it convenient to prescind from its volume altogether and consider the lines of force as emanating from a point. Again, he may consider the mass of a body of whatever size or shape *as if* it were concentrated at a certain point, say the center of gravity. At another time he is not concerned with the *medium* through which a force is operating, but only with its effect at a certain distant point. The constant practice of making such abstractions gives rise to a language which not only makes no mention of extended bodies and concrete media, but even seems to deny these. And the success of the calculations has led some scientists to the conviction that in the last analysis and on a sufficiently small scale the ultimate constituents of matter actually have no extension nor any material medium through which they interact upon one another. Still, we cannot be too frequently warned that the language of mathematical physics is not that of ordinary parlance and writers in that field are often misunderstood by outsiders. What they mean and what we understand are frequently two quite different things. Thus, what they mean by a "particle" is not the absolute zero of arithmetic, but a portion of matter whose dimensions are negligible in proportion to the other distances involved in the problem. In problems involving the earth and the polar star, the earth may be considered a "particle." Also their "zero" is often relative zero, that is, it is a limit which is approached in different ways by different orders. Taking all this into consideration, few if any scientists are pure Dynamists.

THE STATE OF THE QUESTION. Pure Dynamism is understood to be expressed in two tenets: (1) that the material universe is made up *solely of forces,* that there is no matter as distinct from force; and

(2) that the sources of these forces are absolutely inextended, equivalent to mathematical points, and that they operate on one another. Tenet (1) we are not concerned with in the present thesis. We have to deal with tenet (2). Hence we are not here disputing the assertion that force may be a substance and the ultimate subject. Our sole purpose is to show that an extended world cannot consist of inextended components, whatever postulates may be made as to their activities. We may grant for the nonce that there is nothing but force in the universe; our contention is that such forces must nevertheless be extended, and cannot operate from point-sources without an existent medium. Without extension either in the source or the medium we must reject the theory.

Thesis 8. Dynamism, of the kind which contends that bodies are ultimately composed of inextended forces, is inadmissible

Argument. Dynamism, as considered here, teaches that the material universe is ultimately made up of point-forces and empty space. But such a doctrine is inadmissible. Therefore . . .

The minor. (a) The reason for the doctrine is not valid. For some, as for Balmes, the reason is the "mystery of the continuum," in particular its indefinite divisibility. But in Theses 6 and 7 we have shown that if rightly understood the mystery is far from being a contradiction. Moreover, the mystery is common to all space, whether occupied by matter or not. Hence, since the Dynamists postulate space between the simple entities, they have in

no way avoided their difficulties about the continuum. For others the reason seems to lie in the
fact that we can always consider forces as centered
at certain points. In doing so we abstract from the
extent of the body concerned. But it is false to
suppose that abstraction is denial. These centers of
forces are, furthermore, merely a convenient fiction.
For example, were I to determine the center of
gravity of all the ponderable matter in the earth,
and do so with extreme accuracy, I would in all
probability fix upon a point where there is not any
ponderable matter at all, i.e., in the intra-atomic
ether; for we know that only a very small portion of the volume of any body is occupied by ponderable matter. Or I might even suppose that the
point I settle upon is in a total vacuum unoccupied
by anything whatever. If then I say that the whole
earth may be considered as at this point, I surely cannot mean that it is where it is not.

(b) *The interaction of forces requires an existent
medium.* All experimental science rejects as physically impossible the action of a material force
through a total vacuum. (It is not pertinent here
to discuss the metaphysical impossibility of action
at a distance.)

Topics for Discussion. The electrical theory of
matter. Difference between force and extension, or
what makes matter take up room, and what makes
it "go"? Criticize: "Matter is nothing more than
energy in an extremely condensed form and endowed
with a special structure." A. Berthoud, *New Theories of Matter and the Atom* (Macmillan), p. 101.

REFERENCES

Baschab, C. *Manual of Neo-Scholastic Philosophy,* part 1.
Cath. Ency. "Dynamism."
Nys, D. In *Manual of Modern Scholastic Philosophy,*
Vol. 1, parts 3, 4.

CHAPTER IX

THE ESSENCE OF CORPOREAL SUBSTANCE [1]

SUBSTANCE AND QUANTITY. *Descartes* held that
the essence of bodily substance is extension.[2] The
greatest objection to this opinion is that actual extension is an accident and not anything substantial.
Aristotle was well aware of this difficulty, for he
says [3] "Length, breadth, and depth are quantities
and not substances. Quantity is not a substance;
but the substance is rather that to which these things
primarily belong." In order therefore to understand intimately the nature of material substance
we must discuss its relation to quantity.

EXTENSION. "Quantity" is frequently used to
designate the mass or weight of a body, or some
form of energy. In the present thesis we are not
concerned with quantity in that sense. By quantity
we here mean *extension,* pure and simple. Extension, as applied to bodies, implies parts outside of
parts in three-dimensional space, every assignable
part being as truly extended as the total body,
though smaller in size. That is what we mean by
the term "actual local extension."

PROPER AND CONTINGENT ACCIDENTS. We hold
that actual local extension is an accident, and not

---

[1] This thesis may be reserved for a more advanced course.
[2] *Principia phil.* II. 64.
[3] *Metaph.* VI. 3.

a substantial constituent of the body. But it is most important to emphasize the differences between two classes of accidents—proper accidents and contingent (or logical) accidents. A contingent accident is as much a real existing physical entity as is a proper accident; in that they do not differ. But a *proper accident* is one which has a necessary connection with the substantial essence, and is said to flow, follow or emanate from that essence. A common example of proper accident is the power of laughter in man, or the power of speech; these follow from the essential constitution of a rational animal. A *contingent accident* is one which has no necessary connection with the substantial essence. Thus the act of walking is a contingent accident, for a man may be walking or not without detracting from his essence as a man. But it is to be noted that, since a proper accident flows from the essence, there must be something in the very essence itself which demands the presence of the accident. This something is the radix of the proper accident.

ANALYSIS OF CORPOREAL SUBSTANCE. The explanation of corporeal substance advanced here is to the following effect. Actual local extension is a proprium, a proper accident of all bodies. The root-source or radix of extension, as of any proprium, must be in the very essence of the bodily substance. Now the constituent substantial essence of a being is denominated by the genus and specific difference. The highest genus of all is substance; and this is divided into body and spirit. The specific difference which discriminates body from spirit is indicated by declaring that a body has integral parts, whereas a spirit has no such parts. Briefly, then, the *genus* is substance; the *specific difference* is the having integral parts; the two together constitute the proximate *species,* body. All this is on the order of substance; these are substantial characteristics; for the constituent essence of a being does not admit an accident as a component. Genus and specific difference, or, in one word, species, express only substantial components. But the next step brings us to the *proprium,* which is admittedly an accident, though one which necessarily results from the substantial essence. This we maintain is actual extension. For *contingent accidents* in the case of bodies we have position, location, etc. This analysis underlies our contention in the present thesis.

THE ESSENCE OF "BODY." By quantity we understand extension, and not an amount or measure of force. But actual local extension has its root-cause within the substance itself. Hence this root-cause can also be called quantity in some sense, and we call it *internal quantity;* whereas the actual local extension is the *external quantity.* Internal quantity pertains to the very constituent substantial essence of a body; it is the radix of the proprium, external quantity. Our contention is that it is *not inconceivable* that a body should be without actual local extension. We do not maintain that it could, even conceivably, be without internal quantity, for then it should lack something of its very essence, which were absurd. Nor do we wish to imply that our senses could perceive a body without its having local extension. We cannot even form a phantasm of such a body, for our phantasms are extended images of extended objects. But by analysis of the nature of corporeal substance we can form a *concept* which represents body, without including the note of actual local extension. In other words, contrary to Descartes, we hold that actual local extension is not absolutely essential to a body.

Thesis 9. It cannot be shown that actual local extension is absolutely essential to a body

Argument. If actual local extension is absolutely essential to a body it is so either because (1) the two are identical, or (2) the union of the two is absolutely necessary. But neither of these alternatives can be shown to be true; therefore it cannot be shown that actual local extension is absolutely essential to a body.

The major. No other reason can be assigned why actual extension should be included in the essence of body.

The minor. (1) The having of integral parts is a different thing in concept from the expansion of such parts in space. A body is a being having integral parts, which parts have an aptitude and an exigency to be deployed in space. This fact accurately distinguishes a body from a spirit. A spirit may indeed "occupy" space, but it does not do so in the same manner as a body. Thus the soul is present in the human body, but its presence is not by way of parts outside of parts, for the soul has no parts. In whatever part of the body it may be said to be present, it is not partially present there, but totally present, as the vivifying formal cause. This is what is called "definitive presence." But a body occupies space by "circumscriptive presence"; its several parts exclude the other parts from that place, and the whole body is not present in every part of the space occupied. Now, we maintain in this argument that it is not inconceivable that a body should be *de facto* inextended; but even in that state it is not a spirit, for it has the aptitude and the exigency to occupy space circumscriptively; which is precisely what a spirit cannot do. Hence the absolutely essential note which constitutes a body as distinct from spirit is not actual extension, but the aptitude for it. But, since aptitude must precede the act, and since the very aptitude by itself constitutes the being a body, therefore the being is already a body before the fact of extension. That being the case, body and actual local extension are not identical.

(2) We grant that actual extension, being a proprium, emanates from corporeal essence with natural necessity. But we contend that that necessity is only physical, and not absolute. We cannot, it is true, by all the forces at our command deprive utterly of extension any body whatever. But that shows that the necessity is physical. It does not show that the necessity is absolute. An absolutely necessary union is had when the concept of one entity cannot be separated from the concept of the other. But that is not the case here, for we have shown in the first part of this proof that the concept of body is not identical with that of actual extension. Consequently, there is no repugnance in supposing that divine power, which can overcome physical necessity, may reduce a body to an inextended state. That

is what we mean by saying that the union of the two is not absolutely necessary.

Difficulties. 1. A body is defined as an extended substance.

Reply. That definition is a descriptive definition. A descriptive definition does not name the parts which constitute the essence of the thing defined, but instead it names one or more propria, or properties, that are specific. But since extension is a property, or "attribute," of all bodies, corporeal substance is correctly defined, descriptively, as "extended." And even if the body were deprived of extension, that property is still indicated in the aptitude and exigency for extension. The essential definition of body is: a substance having integral parts.

2. A body is a quantified substance.

Reply. Quantity has two meanings: (1) integral parts with aptitude for extension, and (2) actual expansion. In order that a substance be corporeal it is necessary that it be quantified in at least the first sense. It is not absolutely necessary that it be quantified in the second sense.

The Formal Effect of Quantity

We accept Aristotle's division of causes: efficient, material, formal and final. Each cause must have some assignable effect. The effect of a formal cause is called a "formal effect." Quantity is a formal cause, and therefore must have some formal effect. A formal cause does not produce its effect by activity, but by its union with the subject, *inessendo* as the Scholastics phrased it. The presence of a formal cause in a subject is evinced by its effect, by some character of the subject. What then is the character of bodily substance which can be said to be the formal effect of quantity? It was noted above [4] that quantity has a twofold character, one an aptitude and the other its fulfillment. Both of these characters are formal effects of quantity: the aptitude is the primary effect, the actual extension is the secondary effect. The primary effect is "internal quantity," the secondary effect is "external quantity."

Philosophers have waged a great dispute about what the primary formal effect precisely consists in. Several items enter into this primary effect: (1) the entitative (integral) parts themselves, (2) the union of the parts, (3) the order of the parts, (4) the aptitude or exigency for extension. Some have espoused one item, some another, as holding the primacy. It seems sufficient to hold the last named, since it implies all the rest, and still stops short of actual extension. This aptitude is itself an *actus,* and at the same time a *potentia* with respect to actual local extension. Actual local extension is thus the secondary formal effect. Subsequent to this come spatial divisibility, measurability and impenetrability.

Multilocation

Hagiographers narrate that some holy men have been seen to be present in distant places at the same time. Supposing the instances to be true, there is no need for any very recondite explanation of such phenomena. It seems sufficient to say that the man in question was actually in one place only, and that apparitions of him occurred elsewhere. Again, it

[4] Reply to Obj. 2.

does not appear to be impossible for the same soul to actuate a second body. Either of these explanations obviates the difficulty of strict multilocation. Multilocation is of three kinds: *definitive, circumscriptive,* and *mixed.* Definitive multilocation is the simultaneous presence of a spirit, or inextended being, in two or more totally separate places. Circumscriptive is that of an extended body; and mixed is that of a body extended in one place only, and present in an inextended manner elsewhere. Philosophers agree that definitive replication, or multilocation, is possible at least by miracle. As regards circumscriptive replication, a great many Scholastic philosophers, including St. Thomas, deny that it is possible even by miracle.[5] Mixed multilocation, however, cannot be shown to be contradictory; hence we cannot deny that it is possible by miracle. It is this kind of multilocation which most Catholic theologians hold to be the case in the Blessed Sacrament.

Compenetration

Compenetration of bodies, in a loose sense, is a common phenomenon. Thus water may compenetrate a sponge, or a block of wood. This is due to the fact that ordinary "solid" bodies are really porous. But compenetration in the strict sense is quite a different matter. It means the presence together of two *absolutely solid* bodies in the same place. Let us suppose two such bodies each in the form of a cube of the same size as the other. The question is, Can these two bodies, each retaining its identity, occupy exactly the same space? There does

[5] *Quodl.* 3. a.2.

not seem to be any reason why we should hesitate to answer No. Certain miracles have been interpreted by some as requiring compenetration; e.g., the risen Savior's passing through the stone of the sepulcher, and through the closed door of the Cenacle. Aside from the fact that Christ's body was then glorified and "spiritualized" (and about the properties of such a body we know little), there is the very obvious fact that even a mortal human body is extremely porous, and though a miracle would be required for it to pass through a wood or stone barrier, the miracle need by no means be that of compenctration. In any case there is no evidence to show that there was no displacement and reunion of the materials in the barriers.

Topics for Discussion. Definitive presence and omnipresence. Does the expansion and contraction of bodies (e.g., of iron) afford a foundation for the distinction between corporeal substance and its extension? The predicament "quantum" and the predicable "proprium" as applied to bodies. The trustworthiness of the accounts of the bilocation of St. Francis Xavier and St. Alphonsus.

REFERENCES

Cath. Ency., Vol. 5, p. 581. "Bilocation." "Speculative Discussion of Real Presence."

Moreux, Abbé. *What Shall We Become after Death?* Chs. 1-9.

O'Neill, J. *Cosmology,* Ch. 7.

CHAPTER X

SPACE

SCOPE OF THE THESIS. The word "space" is in daily usage among men, and every one readily understands what is meant by it. A printer will speak of space for an article, the captain of a ship will say there is space for so much cargo in the hold of the vessel, a taxicab driver can accurately judge the space needed for his car to slip between two vehicles or the amount of room required to park it at the curb. The vacationist seeks the great open spaces of the country, and the astronomer studies the heavenly bodies immersed in an illimitable sea of space. Even children understand what is meant by space. Still, very few people, if asked, could give an exact definition of the term. The space we speak of in the thesis is not different from that of everyday usage; and our purpose is simply *to defend the definition* there set down.

GENESIS OF THE NOTION OF SPACE. Kant held that the notion of space is a part of the mental equipment with which we come into the world. But that conclusion of his was a result of self-deception. The error occurs in the following manner. I reflect that I always see bodies, and think of them, as *in space;* they occupy space, they are each contained in just so much space, they are surrounded by space, they are immersed in space, and if they move there must be ahead of them ready and waiting a space into which to move. But if the notion of space thus antecedes the most direct sense perception, that notion must be innate. The deception comes from supposing that we have *always,* even from our earliest infancy, perceived bodies as in space, and that we *cannot* perceive them, or think of them otherwise. A little analysis of the data of consciousness will reveal the fact that the notion of space is not the first item, as Kant supposed, but the third. The first perception is that of extended bodies, which we become aware of by their color, or their resistance, and by our own movement about or among them. The next mental act is to make an abstraction. We prescind from their hardness or softness, their smoothness or roughness, their color, and all such qualities, and concentrate our attention upon their extent. We now have arrived at the notion of abstract extension, but this is not as yet "space." We have achieved a representation of extension from which all existing and individual bodies are obliterated, of extension as something standing alone by itself and independent of all bodies. The third operation is to restore the bodies to the expanse from which they have been banished. It is only then that we think of bodies as *in space*. But the whole completed operation is so much a matter of habit in adult life that we are apt to overlook the fact that it contains three distinct mental acts instead of one. The seeing of bodies in space is so far from being a primitive fact of consciousness that it is really the last of the trio. The direct perception of bodies does not suppose the notion of space, but is two removes in advance of that notion.

THE DEFINITION AND THE PHANTASMS. Our *definition* therefore is that *space is abstract extension considered as a receptacle for bodies.* The *phantasms* which one may form to attend this concept will, of course, be various. In order to imagine anything I must fancy it endowed with *some sensible property,* with color, smoothness, cold, etc. Thus I can picture the vast interstellar spaces as having the cerulean tint of the sky. Or I can liken space to an immense sea in which bodies near and far are immersed and move about. If I restrict my consideration to a single body, I can still consider the space which that body alone occupies, and can represent the space as a container, or box, with extremely thin sides; or, better, as some kind of absorbent entity, which instead of moving out of the way for bodies, swallows them up, so to speak, drinks them in and completely engrosses them. Different persons will form different material images, but the underlying notion is that space is a container or receptacle for bodies.

KINDS OF SPACE. Space is divided into *real* space, *possible* space and *absolute* space. Real space is that which is occupied by a body, or bodies. Possible space is unoccupied space. Absolute space is the sum of the two. Hence absolute space takes in all space. We form this notion by prescinding from whether the space be occupied or not, and consider it only as being capable of occupation; in absolute space we break down the barriers between real and possible space and view it all as one. And, whereas real space is limited by the confines of the bodies in existence, and possible space is excluded from the compass of those bodies, absolute space recognizes no limits whatever, and expands indefinitely in all directions. It corresponds to the "infinite" of mathematics. On the other hand, possible space may be very restricted; for if there are vacua within the universe, little volumes not occupied by any matter whatsoever—not even by the ether—these vacua are as truly possible space as that which begins at the outer rim of the universe and stretches from there on illimitably. Real space is always coterminous with the body concerned.

PURE SPACE. In the science of geometry space is regarded somewhat differently from the way it is regarded in the present thesis. Firstly, in mathematics space is considered in one, two or three dimensions; in this thesis we consider it in three dimensions only. It is clear that a body cannot occupy any but three-dimensional space. Secondly, geometry does not regard even its three-dimensional space as being occupied at all; in fact it prescinds from the whole question of occupation by bodies. Nevertheless, this abstention from any reference to occupation does not make geometric space identical with absolute space; for absolute space has no divisions nor any boundaries within or without, whereas geometric space is divided and bounded at will. The explanation is simply this: to form the notion of *geometric space* we abstract the note of extension from the bodies around us, and consider that extension in itself; we stop short of the third mental act necessary to give us the concept of space with which we are concerned in this thesis. Geometric space is also called "pure space" because of its total disassociation from bodies.

OPPONENTS OF THE THESIS. *Clarke,* in a controversy with Leibnitz, defended space as a real existent being, uncreated and divine, in short the immensity of God. *Fénelon* and *Bayma* (and even Newton at times) appear to lean toward the same opinion. *Gassendi* taught that space is an existing being, unique in its kind, halfway between body and spirit, and neither substance nor accident. *Kant* called space a sense-form, not derived from sensation but preceding it. *Descartes* maintained that there is no space apart from the actual extended body, and that extension constitutes corporeal substance.

Thesis 10. Space is abstract extension considered as a receptacle for bodies; hence space as such is a product of the mind, but with a foundation in external reality

Part I (a) Space is abstract extension

Argument. Expansion in three dimensions is a note which is essential to the common concept of space, while other properties such as color, resistance, temperature, or forces of any kind, do not enter into the concept. But expanse represented without the other common and sensible properties of bodies is abstract extension. Therefore space is abstract extension.

Part I (b) This extension is considered as a receptacle for bodies

Argument. That which is considered as filled with bodies or void of bodies, that in which bodies are said to be contained and move about, is considered as a receptacle for bodies. But we so consider the expanse which we call space. Therefore space is abstract extension considered as a receptacle for bodies.

Part II (a) Space is a product of the mind

That is called a product of the mind which is represented as an existing being but which in itself cannot exist. But space as such is represented as if it were an existing being, whereas it cannot as such exist by itself. Therefore space as such is a product of the mind.

Part II (b) This mental product has a foundation in external reality

A mental representation is said to have a foundation in external reality when there actually exists in the concrete state something which corresponds to the representation, although it does not exist in the abstract condition in which it is represented by the mind. Now there exist bodies with the concrete attribute of extension, and it is this attribute which is represented in an abstract manner in the notion of space as such.

Therefore space as such is a product of the mind with a foundation in external reality.

Difficulties. 1. Space is self-existent, eternal, independent of everything else.

Reply. Space we thus represent to ourselves, I grant. That space as such is a real existing being with the attributes mentioned, I deny. These attributes, if they were those of a being existing in itself and independently of the mind, would identify space with God. Aside from the response given it may be noted that space is divisible, and infinitely so; hence it could not possibly be divine. Again it is absurd to say that God is an extended being.

2. Space is infinite in extent.

Reply. Space is conceived as indefinitely great in extent, I concede. It is actually infinite, I deny. Since space is not a thing existing in itself, it has only that extent which we give it by our minds; but our minds cannot picture actually infinite extent. We define absolute space as conceivably extending beyond any limit you may assign; that makes it indefinitely great but not actually infinite.

3. Before the world was created space existed.

Reply. That there actually existed antecedent to the material world any real extended being, I deny. That it was possible for an extended being to exist, I grant. Unoccupied space is in no sense a being existing in itself. Space as such, as we have seen, exists only in the mind. The foundation does actually exist in itself, it is the actually existing body. Real space merely connotes that the space we have in mind is occupied. Possible space means that it is unoccupied.

4. A man at the outer rim of the universe could thrust out his arm. But there must be something there into which to thrust it. Therefore space is an existent something distinct from bodies.[1]

[1] Cf. Locke, *Essay Conc. Hum. Underst.,* II, 13, § 21.

Reply. We *picture* him as thrusting the arm into a sea as it were of space, I grant. He *actually* thrusts his arm *into* anything, I deny. And if you ask what could the man *see* beyond him, we answer, "Simply nothing"; for there is nothing there to see.

5. We say that bodies fill space; but they cannot fill unless there be something to fill.

Reply. We picture them as doing so, but we do not mean that the filling is real outside the mind. Otherwise the thing filled should itself fill space, and that fill another space, and so on forever.

6. Particular spaces have a shape of their own.

Reply. The shape is that of the body occupying the space, or that formed by the bodies surrounding it.

Place

Internal place is the space occupied by a body. External place is the location of a body with reference to other bodies around it. This is what we commonly mean by "place," for when we determine *where* a body is we determine its location with reference to other bodies. Though space is involved in the concept of place, the two are not identical. Space may be considered as divided up into certain sections or volumes, and any one of these volumes may be considered in itself without reference to what is around it. By place we also mean a certain volume of space, which volume is occupied, or occupiable, by a body; but we furthermore consider this portion of space *in reference to what is around it.* Therefore *place is a limited portion of space considered in reference to its position in an extended field.*

Extension in the concrete is a real existing entity,

a physical accident of bodily substance. But it is an absolute accident, not a relative accident. An absolute accident complements its subject by itself, and without any necessary reference to others. For example, health is an absolute accident. A relative accident is a complement which a substance has on account of some other being or beings; as, for example, friendship. Now, extension is possessed by a body independently of any other body; and if all the other bodies were annihilated, extension would still be possessed by the body remaining. Size, on the other hand, is a relative accident, for it depends on a comparison with other bodies; and if all bodies but one were annihilated, the remaining one, though it have real extension, cannot be said to have size. Nor would the remaining body have real place, for *place is a relative accident*. We can of course imagine other bodies in the vicinity of the lone existing body, but these imaginary bodies can neither be the subject nor the terminus of a real relation.

Briefly, then, just as imaginary space (i.e., possible space) denies the presence of bodies, so real space asserts the presence of extended matter. Place, however, since it is a relationship, ceases to be real as soon as either the terminus or the subject is rendered unreal. Likewise, of course, if both are unreal.

Let us fasten our attention on real, existing bodies, and then ask what is the meaning of place. We answer that place is a real, existing, relative accident. A body's location is determined by the bodies around it. But it is necessary that the surrounding bodies be at rest. Hence Aristotle defined place as "the immobile surface of the surrounding matter." [2]   If, for instance, the surface of water where it is in contact with the fish it encloses, does not move, the fish has a fixed place; but if the fish swim, or the water flow by him, he has no fixed place with reference to the water.   We need not, however, confine the determination of place within such narrow limits as the Stagirite selected.   We can determine place from bodies more remote than those in the immediate vicinity.

The ultimate foundation for the relationship of place is extension.   Extension gives a meaning to direction and distance, and these latter are the proximate foundation for that position in an extended field, which we call "place."   Thus, without actual contact, a body's location is its distance and direction from a given stationary body.   In this manner we determine the position of a vessel at sea from some fixed point or points on the coast.

Motion

Real place, as we have seen, is a fixed unvarying relationship between a given body and some other body or bodies.   But a body may change this relationship by departing from one place and going to another.   This is what we call motion. In considering motion here we are not concerned with the cause of motion.   Nor are we concerned with the effect which a moving body may produce in another body which happens to be in its path.   We are merely studying the nature of *local motion as such*.   What then is motion?   *Mo-*

[2] *Phys.* IV. 4.

tion is a continuous change of place. We say it is continuous because, if a body simply went out of existence in one place and came into existence again at another, the change would be discontinuous and abrupt, it would not be motion; it would be an exchange instead of a change of position. Motion must be *gradual.* By that we do not mean that it must be slow, nor that its speed must be uniform. Speed and acceleration are not essentially involved in the motion as such. By being gradual we mean that (1) there is no section of its path, however small, at which the body came to rest, and (2) that the sections were passed over successively and not simultaneously. (Acceleration may also be gradual; and although the term "instantaneous velocity" is used in dealing with acceleration, what is meant is that a sufficiently brief moment is taken to enable us to neglect the change of velocity, or the acceleration, in that moment.)

The motion of a body is, therefore, "formally" motion as long as the body continues to move at all; and this motion does not terminate except in total rest. When rest ensues the body occupies a fixed place. But since place is relative to the field about it, so also are rest and motion relative to that field. This does not mean that these things are not real; they are indeed very real accidents, and they belong to the category called relation.

Non-Euclidian Space

Saccheri, using the diagram given below, sets down the following proposition: Given AC and BD perpendicular to AB, and given AC equal

to BD; then the line CD will be equal to AB if the
enclosed angles at C and D are right angles, but CD
will be greater than AB if those angles are obtuse,
and less if they are acute.   It is clear from the
proposition that Saccheri, instead of accepting the
parallel postulate as self-evident, is about to make
an attempt to prove it.   To all appearances he did
prove that the angles at C and D cannot be other
than right angles.   Still, mathematicians are not
altogether convinced that his proof is valid.   This
does not mean that they doubt the truth of Saccheri's
conclusion; for we may accept a conclusion, and at
the same time doubt the validity of a particular
proof for it.   Hence mathematicians are still seek-
ing to discover whether the parallel postulate can
be established by formal proof, or must be accepted
as evident in itself.

Meanwhile, some mathematicians have chosen to
assume that the angles at C and D are obtuse, others
that they are acute.   And on one or other supposition they have built up two kinds of geometry which
are certainly not Euclidian.   Granted the original
assumptions, these geometries are as truly systems
of consistent reasoning as is the reasoning of Euclidian geometry.   The whole question is whether the
non-Euclidian geometry is verified in the actual material world.   If we abandon the parallel postulate
as not being self-evident, and as not being capable
of proof by geometric methods, then our only hope
of establishing it is by actual measurement.
Although physical measurement is an imperfect
means, it has been attempted on a large scale; but
never have the measurements shown space to be

other than Euclidian. From whatever source we derive our assurance, there is a deep-seated conviction in all of us that actual space cannot be anything but Euclidian, and that, therefore, non-Euclidian space is simply a mathematical deduction from an unreal hypothesis.[2]

Topics for Discussion. Geometric space as compared to the common meaning of space. How we acquire the notion of space as such. The possibility of vacua in the universe. Does the displacement of stars around the eclipsed sun prove that space is "curved"?

REFERENCES

Cath. Ency. "Space."

Moreux, Abbé. *What Shall We Become After Death?* Chs. 5, 6, 7.

Nys, D. In *Manual of Modern Scholastic Philosophy.* "Cosmology," Appendix, art. 2.

O'Neill, J. *Cosmology.* Vol. 1, Ch. 9.

Rickaby, J. *General Metaphysics,* p. 368.

[2] The question of time as a fourth dimension is taken up at the end of thesis eleven.

CHAPTER XI

TIME

MOTION AS A BASIS FOR TIME. It was St. Augustine who said: "What is time then? If nobody asks me, I know: but if I were desirous to explain it to one that should ask me, plainly I know not." [1] But the saint's modesty induced him to underrate his comprehension of this difficult subject. Still the term "time," so frequently used and so readily understood in everyday life, has proved a conundrum to many a philosopher who attempted to define it. The principal source of the difficulty would seem to be the *non-existence* of the *future,* and, for that matter, of the *past* as well. And when we consider that the future and the past are separated only by a "knife-edge," in Professor James' phase, the very *present* is reduced to zero, and the whole of time appears to vanish. In attacking this difficulty, we have in the statement of our thesis introduced *local motion as the basis* of our concept of time. The reason is that motion supposes an extended field. Now, extension is a matter of very obvious sense perception and is easily comprehended as a fact. In particular it is free from the special difficulty which clings to time, namely its seeming to perish just as it comes into being. The existence of one part of extension

[1] *Conf.* 11, 14.

does not exclude the existence of the other parts. Extension is therefore called a "permanent continuum," as opposed to "successive continuum." Then, given extension, motion becomes intelligible. And, although motion, being a continuous change of place, is a successive continuum, it at least has this advantage over time that it is a *visible phenomenon*. Moreover, its path, or its "past," so to speak, can in some manner be taken in by the eye; the moving object may leave a track behind it, as the wake of a vessel, or footprints in the snow, or the line drawn by a moving piece of chalk; and, failing that, the eye can easily span the distance between the moving body and some point which it has passed over. Likewise, the driver of a car keeps in view both the section of road which he has passed over and that which is immediately before him. Thus, while motion is actually taking place at one point only, the very existence of the road or path enables the mind to give a kind of existence to movement along the entire course. Extension gives to the successive continuum motion, a "before" and an "after"; then with motion so equipped, we find it relatively easy to pass on to the concept of time.

DIFFERENCE BETWEEN TIME AND MOTION. Time, however, though based on physical motion, is not identical with it. It is true that both time and motion have direction; but the direction of motion is reversible, while that of time is not. A motion when it is reversed may be said to subtract what it had added up; time never subtracts; it can only add, it is *irreversible*, it cannot but go forward. Again, motion can vary its speed; the advance of time is essentially *uniform*. The pendulum is subject to continuous acceleration, but the time moves evenly onward. If we choose the earth's motion about its axis, that motion is indeed regarded as uniform but it brings us back daily to a point where the sun is on the meridian; we have not however returned to the same point of time but are forever carried farther along time's endless course. *Irreversibility* is therefore a note which time does not share with motion. As regards the rate of time's change, it must be admitted that in order to endow time with the character of *uniformity,* we must first select some motion as a standard, e.g., the motion of the earth. Now, the idea of a standard is that it does not vary. The selection of any motion as a standard makes it qualify as perfectly uniform motion. The standard is essentially invariable, all other motions may be variable. Having thus built up the notion of time as *uniform motion in one direction,* we proceed, by mental prescision, to separate this constant forward movement from any necessary association with a particular body, and thus *we represent time as something apart* by itself, a great forward-going, even-moving stream, by whose rate of change all other rates are measured. We have then arrived at the concept of time as such.

ARISTOTLE'S DEFINITION. Aristotle's famous definition of time, *"Numerus motus secundum prius et posterius"* [2] may be rendered, "The reckoning of motion as previous and subsequent." As we have noted above, motion as such may repeat itself; but in order for it to enter into the concept of time, it

[2] *Phys.* IV. 11.

must not be considered as repeating. Consequently, for this purpose we image the motion as proceeding along a straight line. We can then divide it into sections, "number" it as Aristotle says; and every section is before (*prius*), or after (*posterius*) some other section. The grand division of time is of course into past and future. Any point you select anywhere in the whole course of time, will have a future and a past, a "before" and an "after." And any section you take will be previous to and subsequent to other sections; days, hours, seconds are all set out in a series of "before and after." We might therefore, paraphrase the definition thus: Time is the counting, or telling off, of motion in an irreversible series. The fact that Aristotle calls time a "numbering," and, afterwards, a "measure," is sufficient to show that he was aware of its being used as a standard, and consequently uniform.

KINDS OF TIME. Time is divided by some authors into intrinsic and extrinsic. *Intrinsic time* is said to be the duration of any particular motion as the thing measured; thus a runner's time for the hundred yards may be given as ten seconds; the duration of the run, his "time," is in this case not the measure of anything else, but the thing measured. His time may be shorter or longer on the next run. The *measure* is the earth's motion (indicated by the stop-watch), and does not vary. Evidently, we are not in this thesis dealing with intrinsic time. *Extrinsic time* is a standard rate of change which is used as the measure of the duration of other things. It is the definition of extrinsic time that we are defending here. Time is also denominated real, possible and absolute. *Real time* is that which coincides with the actual changes in the material universe; it extends from the beginning of motion up to the actual present, and is constantly being added to. *Possible time* is that which is not coincident with actual motion; it embraces not only the future but also that imaginary time which preceded the beginning of motion in the universe. *Absolute time* is both real and possible time considered as one; it is therefore all time, prescinding from whether or not it have the concomitant of existing physical motion. The terms "absolute time" and "imaginary time" are frequently used to express the fact that we think of time as independent of any moving body whatever, as not being moored to any object in the universe, but keeping to its own serene, unhurried, unflagging course, let all moving bodies vary as they may. But that is nothing else than the concept of *time as such,* the concept which we shall prove to be correctly defined in the statement of our thesis; it is time as distinguished from quantitative and qualitative changes, and is verified in real, possible and absolute time. In this we see the analogy between time and space; each of the ideas is formed by seizing upon a phenomenon of bodies, then abstracting that phenomenon from the body, taking it away, and representing it as something existing apart by itself. Having done this we proceed to make each a container or measure of real or possible worlds; but while things are contained in space by occupying it, they are contained in time by coexisting with it.

OPPONENTS OF THE THESIS. *Clarke,* who in his

controversy with Leibnitz confused space with the immensity of God, likewise identifies time with the divine eternity. But since there can be no succession or divisibility in God, Clarke's contention must be rejected. *Kant* taught that time is a mental "form" innate in some internal sense faculty. As with space, so he mistakes the derived idea, time, for a supposed "form" which antedates our earliest sense experience. A careful analysis of the data, however, discloses the fact that the experience of change must precede the concept of time. *Lotze* and his followers admit that there is on the part of the object some correspondence to our representation of time, but they deny that there is any real succession, and concede only virtual and analogous succession. This modified Kantianism is much in favor in certain circles. It is an attempt to unite idealism and realism into one doctrine, and must end in error. *Bergson,* who disdains exact definitions and consistency of terminology and appeals only to our powers of intuition, is not too clear about his own intuition of time. He seems to reduce the whole of time to the conscious present. There is no future, no past, and the present is almost nothing. The entire world rolls up its past into the present, which has scarcely more than the thickness of a mathematical plane. Surely the adequate concept of time disappears in this "intuition." Many scientific and philosophical writers, as, e.g., *Einstein,* confound the notion of time with the difficulties we experience in measuring it, and in determining simultaneity. In ancient times, *Epicurus,* an out-and-out materialist,

taught that time as such had an independent existence
outside the mind.

*Thesis 11. Time is continuous movement consid-
ered as a measure of the duration of other
things; time as such is, therefore, like space, a
product of the mind with a foundation in objective fact*

Part I

Argument. Time is (a) a constant succession,
(b) to which other beings are referred as coexistent.
But this is (a) continuous movement, (b) considered as a measure of the duration of other things.
Therefore . . .

The major. (a) Time is essentially uninterrupted
progression. Every assignable part, however small,
follows another part; and that, without the slightest
break, or gap, in the course. (b) There is nothing
which we cannot declare to be coexistent with some
section or some point of time. The Roman Empire
lasted through a certain span of years; the first shot
in the war was fired at a certain moment, etc.

The minor. (a) Constant succession of the kind
described above can be nothing but continuous
change. It is continuous because indefinitely divisible, and it is change because the parts are consecu-
tive. The term "movement" is intended to express
change of any kind, whether qualitative or quantitative, but it is especially appropriate in defining
time, since time is usually associated with local motion; as, for example, the diurnal rotation of the

earth. (b) The coexistence of things with some stretch of time is our reason for saying they are contained in that time. Thus the events of a day are so called because they coexisted with that day; it is the day that sets them apart and measures them off as distinct from preceding and subsequent events. The duration, or "lifetime," of every mundane thing is enclosed in a certain span of time; and there is always enough time to serve as a measure. Be the thing great or small, time never fails to have an exact fit for it.

Part II (a) Time is a product of the mind

Argument. Time is conceived as an entity subsisting in itself and with its own fixed rate of advance. But such an entity is a product of the mind.

The major. We shall illustrate our concept of time by what is probably a common enough phantasm. We picture a mighty river ceaselessly flowing toward us; as it passes, this stream carries away with it an indelible record of what it finds.

The minor. But there is no such entity; for it should have to be disembodied motion, subsisting in itself, without any moving thing of which it was the motion, and without any reason for its uniform rate. Hence, time as such is a product of the mind.

Part II (b) Time as such has a foundation in objective fact

Argument. Motion is something real and existing independently of the mind. But motion is the foundation of time. Therefore time as such has a foundation in objective fact.

The major. Movements in the world take place whether we think about them or not, or know about them.

The minor. Though everything be in motion (at least with the motion of the earth) there is this salient fact that moving things do not all stay together in space. Thus, if while a man is walking his hat blows off, though the man and the hat continue to move they do not remain together; and a passing automobile will increase its distance from both the man and the scurrying hat. This phenomenon gives us the idea of *rate* of change. All the rates are in themselves relative to one another; but they offer the possibility for the mind to fasten upon one as a standard, and to reckon all the others in reference to that one. Thus motion becomes the basis of the concept, time.

Difficulties. 1. Time cannot require motion for its foundation, for there was time before there was any world to move.

Reply. We can now, witnesses as we are of motion, picture time as antedating the world in the same way as we picture the future time which the world has not as yet reached. But without motion, or successive change of any kind to experience, we should be bereft of any data with which to begin the formation of the notion of time.

2. There must have been time actually existent before the world, for the world began to exist *in time*.

Reply. The world did not begin to exist in real time,

for that instant was the initial point of real time; nor in possible time, for the instant was exactly between the two. But it was nevertheless *in absolute time*.

3. Motion as such and time as such are hopelessly inseparable, and consequently it is idle to speak of one being the foundation of the other, etc. Consider only this fact: Time means uniform motion. But uniform motion means equal distance *in equal time*. In other words, to arrive at the notion of time I must have uniform motion, but to know whether I have uniform motion I must first have time. Time is measured by motion and motion by time. Such reciprocal measurements make it impossible that time even in concept can be anything different from motion, or vice versa.

Reply. There are three answers possible, each of them a valid defense of our thesis:

(a) The objector speaks of local motion, for he mentions distance. But local motion is not the sole and exclusive basis of time. One can build up a concept of time entirely independently of local motion. Local motion directly involves extension, but there are other continuous changes which do not directly involve extension. These are qualitative changes. If, for example, an iron plate upon which I rest my hand becomes alternately hot and cold, or electrically charged and neutral, or if a screen before me changes from white to black and back again to white, there is in all these experiences no perception of local motion, and any one of them might be employed for the basis of time, as truly as a swinging pendulum.

(b) There is also an internal experience of the lapse of time which is certainly not based on the direct perception of local motion. The musician, for example, has a sense of time, which he may or may not represent by isolated beats, he can lengthen or shorten the intervals between the beats, and be conscious of which he is doing and by how much. Again, a man seated, blindfolded, in a large swing-like pendulum, could have a perception of time from the gradual variations in the experience of gravitation. Or, if the pendulum were to travel along a level path, he would experience the gradual fading of inertia into momentum, and vice versa. In the last two examples, motion is the indirect cause of the experience, but the local motion as such is not perceived.[3] Then, too, the perception of time is involved in the effort we experience in accomplishing a given task. A runner (without counting his steps or calculating the length of his stride) has a sense of time based on the intensity of his effort. And in intelligence tests we are conscious of time by the efforts we make to keep our attention fixed and make mental calculations. In all this it is evident that we are not limited to local motion as the only phenomenon upon which we can base our concept of time.

(c) The uniformity of change is not time's only characteristic. Time is a *comparison* of one rate with another, or others. In order to effect a comparison, one change or movement must be selected as a standard. A standard, *ipso facto,* cannot vary. If I were to select the current of the Mississippi as a standard, then my boat floating with the current must be regarded as uniform motion; while the boat is passing the rapids, the stars should lag in their courses, only to forge ahead when the boat reached a broad lake-like expanse. Hence, we first determine what uniformity means (and we can do so even independently of local motion), then, if we would be most reasonable, we select a standard which by all tests seems to have nearly uniform local motion, e.g., the rotation of the earth; but

[3] Even in determining the uniformity of the earth's motion about its axis we are not confined to measuring the sweep of the meridian across equal portions of the heavens; but we are persuaded that if the rotation notably slowed down or speeded up at certain sections of its course, we and other objects of the earth's surface would have a tendency to fall eastward or westward as the case might be.

once selected it qualifies as uniform, and remains so unless we abandon it for other standards.

4. The only time is the "now," and that has perished as soon as it has begun; therefore there is no such thing as time.

Reply. The "now" is not part of time, as Aristotle long ago noted. It is the equivalent of a point in a line. Such is the "now" considered mathematically. But we do as a matter of fact perceive an actual, and somewhat enduring "now." Sensations linger in the sense faculty even after the exciting impulse has ceased; thus, there are vibrations in the inner ear which go on after the external sound has stopped. If a note is sounded, and after a brief interval a second note of the same pitch and intensity follows, the ear will perceive the second as louder than the first, because the vibration which was left by the first note is taken up and increased by the second. Likewise if the second note is of a different pitch, but in harmony with the first, the experience is pleasant; and unpleasant if the second note is out of harmony. This overlapping of sensations gives us a perception of a present that has some duration. And in ordinary parlance the present means not a point of time, but a section of time; as, for instance, the present hour. Such a present is a part of time.

5. If time may be defined so apodictically as is done in this thesis, why is it that people in general have so much difficulty in expressing what they mean by the term, and in making their expressions agree?

Reply. The principal reason would seem to be that we always dress our concepts in some phantasm or other. The phantasm may suit the concept in one respect but fail in all the others. Thus if I represent time as a road down which we must travel, and can never turn back, I have a phantasm which represents the irreversibility of time and its essential division into a before and after. On another occasion I choose to represent time as something ever marching onward with even tread; but that phantasm will not agree with the one of the road, and so I am confused.

The Various Senses in Which Different Classes of Beings May Be Said to Exist in Time

To exist in time is to coexist with time. But different things coexist with time in different ways. *Bodies* in a state of continuous movement, whether that be local or other change, are *most properly* said to exist in time. That is because uninterrupted and infinitesimal succession is the essence of time; and hence there is always part to part correspondence. This is true regardless of the respective rates at which the bodies change. Changing bodies are therefore most properly said to exist in time, not only because they merely coexist with it, but they *change with* it. They are like a mill-wheel which instead of standing still in the current of time continually revolves with the stream. The changes, however, of which we have been speaking are due to changing accidents. There are other changes in bodies which effect the inner nature, e.g., chemical changes; and these changes are more abrupt; for all practical purposes they are instantaneous. Corporeal *substances,* therefore, maintain a certain fixed character throughout a greater or lesser stretch in the stream of time; and if they change that character, they do so abruptly; they exchange one fixed state for another fixed state. We can thus mark off a section of time in which the corporeal nature *did not change.* The change is not gradual and continuous; the succession comes *in sections*. Corporeal nature is therefore *less properly* said to be in time than continuous change is said to be. This instantaneous change is characteristic not only of the exchange of corporeal nature, but also of the exchange of thoughts and volitions in a spiritual substance. These latter can also endure without any variation in themselves through a certain stretch of time. However, when we come to *spiritual substances,* there is a difference. Two spirits cannot combine to form one new spiritual nature; hence spirits either exist substantially unchanged, or go out of existence altogether. Spiritual substances are, therefore, *still less properly* said to be in time than those entities which are capable merely of abrupt exchanges. Lastly, God is *very improperly* said to be in time; for it is inconceivable that there be in God any succession whatever: neither existence succeeding nonexistence, nor vice versa; nor any exchange of states, as in the case with created spirits. God possesses all His perfections *together*. That is God's eternity. We do not hold with Lotze and his followers that time as applied to the material world is analogous; but we do hold that it is analogous when applied to God. In the terms of ontology, it is an analogy of extrinsic attribution.

The Einstein Theory

Einstein is a great mathematician, and whatever happens to the various interpretations of his mathematics, the mathematics themselves will stand. But many, even including Einstein himself, when making philosophical deductions, have been misled, if not into error, at least into ambiguous statements; and much publicity has been secured by some of these startling assertions. We must confine ourselves here to a simple presentation of the elements of the theory as bearing on the concepts of space and time.

The theory of relativity is twofold, the restricted theory and the general theory. The former concerns uniform motion, the latter accelerated motion.

An example used to illustrate the *restricted theory* is that of a pebble dropped from the window of a uniformly moving train. To the man who released it, the pebble drops in a straight line; to an observer on the ground it describes a parabola. It is a trite observation to say that motion is relative and that its direction depends on the coördinates you refer it to. But it is startling to assert that a straight line may be a curved line. The latter, however, is not true. If the line of fall were marked by chalk on the side of the coach, and by, say, a trail of smoke in the stationary air, then to both observers the first line would be straight and the second curved.

We then proceed to determine simultaneity. At two points, say a kilometer apart, along a straight stretch of the railway, two rifles are fired together. (Einstein illustrates by electric flashes.) As the rifles are fired, midway between the two is an observer on the ground, and one on the moving train. The first will hear the shots together, the second will not. And if you add a third observer on a train going in the opposite direction, his observation will be in reverse order to that of the second. If the rifles be mounted on one of the trains with the three

observers together at the midpoint when the detona-
tions occur, even then neither of the two at the win-
dows will get the reports simultaneously, and the
observer on the ground will notice a slight difference at least in the sharpness, or duration, of the
reports.   Does all this show, as Bergson says,[4] that
simultaneity has no meaning? It certainly does not.
Simultaneity is *supposed* in the giving of the sig-
nals, and it is the very thing we are trying to *measure*.   We must make corrections for the train's
speed. But suppose that instead of sound we are
dealing with light, and with ether instead of air;
then in order to make very exact measurements, I
must know the earth's rate and direction of motion
through the ether.

Michelson and Morley, in the eighties of last
century, tried to determine this motion of the earth,
but failed.[5] To account for the failure of the Michelson-Morley experiment, Lorenz and Fitzgerald,
independently of one another, made the guess, or
assumption, that bodies contract in proportion as
they are turned parallel to the ether-current. What
concerns us here is merely the question: Does this
mean a contraction of space? And we answer, No;
for at most it means only the contraction of bodies.
For example: given two yard-measures crosswise
to the ether-current, their extremities coinciding.
I turn one of them through a right angle; it con-
tracts, it undergoes an internal change. What kind
of change do I mean? I mean that if the second

---

[4] *Durée et simultanéité*, passim.
[5] Professor D. C. Miller claims to have secured some results in
this field, but they are problematical as yet.

yard-measure were of such material as *not* to undergo that change, then when I turned it to the position of the other the extremities would no longer coincide. If all materials contract equally, I cannot perform the experiment; but I still know what equal lengths mean; otherwise, I could not speak of unequal lengths, or changes of length.

A conundrum for the Relativist is a body moving with the speed of light. It must contract to zero thickness. And if it moved faster than light it must somehow turn its thickness inside out. To forfend such possibilities the Relativist maintains that there cannot be any speed greater than that of the electro-magnetic disturbance.

The *generalized theory* of relativity has to do with accelerated motion. Again the observer on the train; the train is "pulling out"; the observer fancies the station has begun to move. Which is really moving? You say at once that the passenger can tell that it is he who is moving, by reason of the inertia of his body. Einstein counters by saying that for all we know some influence may have begun at this moment to pull the earth to the rearward of the train, and that some pull gives the passenger his feeling on inertia. The engineer, by starting the locomotive at the right moment, makes the train stem the tide, and possibly, like a swimmer in a stream, succeeds in merely keeping the train at a standstill. What are we to say to all this? It is perfectly evident that if you select only two objects and compare their motion, their mutual change of position, you may consider either one indifferently as stationary. There is nothing new in that. One can reduce the consideration to motion alone, by limiting the case to two objects and neutralizing the evidence from inertia. But let us suppose another train on the next track and starting out in the opposite direction. The earth must then move in opposite directions at the same time.

Our next problem is gravitation; and we reduce it to inertia in the following manner. A cabinet is located in space remote from all other bodies. The observer within experiences nothing like weight. Then a cable, attached to the roof, begins to pull with accelerated speed. Immediately there is the phenomenon of gravitation within the cabinet. Is, then, gravitation only inertia? The most we can say is that it may be so treated mathematically. But if I suppose the gravitation on the planets to be caused by their accelerated expansion, they had long since begun to swallow one another, and the sun to swallow them all.

In short, if by "space" I mean the *measurement* of space, and if that measurement is affected by motion, and motion involves the factor time, then time is an element of "space," and must enter into my calculations of distance. And if by *time* I mean clocks (as Einstein usually does), I am under superable difficulties about keeping the clocks synchronous at remote distances and under varying conditions. And if "curved space" means a heavy gravitational field, affecting the course of light, it is not nonsense. And so of the rest of the theory.

Topics for Discussion. Solar and sidereal time. Time as a "fourth dimension." The meaning of "now." The Michelson-Morley experiment. Bergson's description of time.

REFERENCES

Cath. Ency. "Time."

Dublin Quart. Review. Vol. 166, p. 256, "Concerning Einstein." Vol. 167, p. 75, "Physical Aspects of Einstein's Principle of Relativity."

Einstein, A. *Meaning of Relativity* (Princ. Univ. Press). *Sidelights on Relativity* (Dutton).

Lorentz, H. *The Einstein Theory of Relativity* (Brentano, N. Y.).

Month. Vol. 143, p. 206, "Einstein and Gravitation." Vol. 134, p. 516, "Einstein vs. Newton."

Nys, D. In *Manual of Modern Scholastic Philosophy.* "Cosmology," Appendix, art. 1.

Scientific Am. Supplement. Vol. 124. Various essays.

Scientific Am. Monthly. Vol. 3, p. 293, "The Einstein Theories." Vol. 3, p. 484, "Planetary Motion and Einstein."

Weyl, H. *Time, Space, Matter* (Dutton).

PART II

THE COMMON PROPERTIES OF BODIES

SECTION 2. ACTIVITY

CHAPTER XII

EFFICIENCY

DEFINITIONS. A *principle* is that from which something else takes its rise. Under the general heading of principle comes cause; but while principle expresses priority, cause signifies a priority of a particular kind. There is an essential connection between the cause and that which follows it, namely, the effect. The effect is not only posterior to the cause, it could never exist without the cause. *Cause* is therefore defined as a *principle to which something else owes its existence.* This is the same as saying that the reason for the existence of the effect is not in the effect itself but in the cause. Thus the existence of motion in a baseball is not due to the ball itself but to the man who threw it. We have previously discussed final cause. We have now to discuss efficient cause. *Efficient cause is that which by its physical activity gives rise to some other entity.* The characteristic of an efficient cause is that its product is due to the physical activity of the agent. Activity is defined by Aristotle [1] as the exercise of a power. In referring to efficient causes we speak of their activity as "physical" in order to distinguish them from final causes which exert their power by an appeal to the intellect and will.

[1] Cf. *Metaph.* XI (X). 9; *Phys.* III. 2.

AN EFFECT IS SOMETHING NEW. It is important to note that the effect is a new entity, it is something that *comes into being,* it did not exist before and exists now. Our opponents in this thesis speak of the occurrences in nature as if they were something handed over intact from one body to another. If in a game of billiards, the cue-ball stopped "dead" and the ball which it struck moved on, our opponents would describe the phenomenon in language which would be equivalent to saying that the motion leaped from the one to the other. We on the other hand say that the motion died down in one body and a new motion arose in the other. We maintain that the motion in the second is an *effect,* and that its rise is due to the activity of the first. We do not explain the events of nature as if they were nothing more than riders that vaulted from one mount to another, or as if they were water poured from one vessel into another. In particular we reject the supposition that motion can exist apart from any moving body, and that this same identical entity can be transferred about, without losing its identity, from vehicle to vehicle. We admit that it is convenient mathematically to abstract from the identity of the motion or other forms of energy and consider only their *equivalent quantity,* but we deny that in the concrete the same physical accident detaches itself from one object and migrates to another.

ENERGY AND MOTION. It is evident that we have here to deal with the great factor called physical energy. *Energy* is defined as the capacity for doing work. Work is the overcoming of resistance, and is measured by the force required times the displacement, W=Fs. Energy is kinetic if it is associated with motion, and potential if associated with position. Kinetic energy is indicated in (1) local motion, e.g., the wind, (2) heat, which is molecular motion, (3) an electric current, or a moving electric charge. Potential energy is the stress, or the strain, of a material system, and may be expressed in terms of attraction or repulsion. Examples of potential energy are (1) gravitation, (2) elasticity, (3) chemical attraction, (4) magnetism, and (5) electrostatic energy (for instance, in the Leyden jar). Radiant energy, e.g., radiant heat, or other similar disturbances of the ether, would seem to be partly kinetic and partly potential, being both motion and strain. The law of *conservation of energy* states that all these types of energy may be converted into one another without loss of capacity for work. This law, of course, supposes that deduction be made for the amount dissipated in heat. We have discussed this dissipation in connection with entropy, but it is necessary to revert to it here for the sake of clearness. "Energy," as defined and divided above, refers to *available energy;* and the law of the conservation of energy concerns that kind of energy primarily, but makes a proviso to cover the amount that is no longer available. The working, therefore, of this law cannot result in indefinitely preserving all the above types as possible; the final outcome will be the one type, heat. When heat has reached an equilibrium, there will be an end of energy understood as a capacity for doing work. The conclusion is that all other types of energy are convertible into heat, but that heat is not *ultimately* convertible into any other type. The reason for pointing out this conclusion is the fact that many writers contend that all the types of energy are some form of motion; and they base their contention on the convertibility of all the other types into the motion which we call heat.

Now, while we readily grant that every release of energy is attended with local motion, nevertheless the sweeping assertion that all energy is motion seems indefensible. We have merely to instance the cases of gravity and elastic strain. And if the term energy be extended to include force, the opinion is still more untenable; for the ultimate particles of matter have cohesion, they resist division: to reduce this ultimate cohesion to mere motion is simply impossible.

ENERGY AND EFFICIENT CAUSE. When an equilibrium of energy is established there is no further change, but it is incorrect to say that all efficient causality has ceased. Even the equilibrium of heat in a closed system supposes the molecules to be imparting motion to one another. Furthermore, a body, without acting at all, still retains the power to act. When such a cause is idle it is said to be *in actu primo,* or in the first stage; when acting it is *in actu secundo*. But in either case it is a cause. If, therefore, energy is restricted to meaning activity (e.g., motion), it is not then coextensive with efficient cause.

DIVERGENT VIEWS. The *Extreme Mechanists,* who reduce all the properties of bodies to quantity and motion,[2] are usually set down as adversaries to this thesis. They, however, admit that one particle of matter can put another particle in motion. Hence they do not deny all efficiency, but rather admit only one kind, namely, momentum. Among the *Energists,* such men as Ostwald frequently speak of energy as if it were a packet of something shifted bodily from one object to another. Berthoud who says, "Matter is nothing more than energy in an extremely condensed form and endowed with a special structure,"[3] at times favors the "transfer," but

[2] E.g., Democritus, Epicurus, Descartes, Secchi.
[3] *New Theories of Matter and the Atom,* p. 101.

when he comes to radiant energy admits the cessation of one kind and the origin of another.[4]   Mor-
gan [5] speaks of causation as "transmission." In general, the theory that "matter" and energy are transmutable has reawakened the fiction that causality
is a migration of entities.[6]   The *Occasionalists*
(Malebranche, etc.), misled by Descartes' definition of substance as applying only to God, asserted
that creatures were the mere occasion, while God
Himself directly produced the effects.   We shall
treat this opinion among the "Difficulties."

STATE OF THE QUESTION. We maintain that
creatures can bring into existence a new being; we
do not, however, by this mean creation.   Creation
is the production of a substance without employing
any subject-matter from which to produce it.   The
efficiency of creatures is not creative but *mutative;*
they must be given a subject in which to produce
the effect.   Again, activity is either immanent or
transient.   Action is immanent when the cause and
the effect are in the same individual, as when a man
lifts his hand.   Action is transient when the effect
occurs outside the agent, as when a man hurls a
stone.   In our argument we shall speak only of
transient action, and restrict that to motion.

*Thesis 12. Natural bodies act with true efficient
causality*

Argument. When a body strikes another the
motion in the latter is either identical with the mo-

[4] *Ibid.,* p. 103.
[5] *Emergent Evolution,* p. 283.
[6] Cf. St. Th., *Sum th.* I. q.115, a.1, ad 5.

tion of the first, or it is new motion.   But it is not identical.

The major.   We admit that the energy gained by the second body is *equivalent* [7] to that lost by the first.   Therefore by "identity" we do not mean equal *amount,* but the *same entity.*

The minor.   Motion is an accident of bodily substance.   But an accident is intrinsically and essentially dependent on substance, hence it cannot pass over as an independent entity from one subject to another.   Therefore the motion of the second body is new.

But this motion would not occur except for the action of the first body.   Therefore the motion of the second body owes its existence to the activity of the first.   In other words, the first acts with true efficient causality.

Since motion is so universally produced in the manner described, according to the contention of our opponents, we can on their own ground conclude against them that: Natural bodies act with true efficient causality.

Difficulties.   1.   Inorganic bodies are inert; but inert bodies are incapable of activity.

Reply.   By saying that a body is inert we mean that it cannot move itself, that is, it cannot change its own state of rest or motion; but it can act on other bodies.   Inorganic bodies are indeed incapable of immanent action; they are, however, capable of transient activity.

2.   God acts most perfectly; but it is more perfect to accomplish a thing oneself than to resort to others for

[7] Allowance being made for diffusion.

coöperation. Therefore God does not permit the participation of creatures in the effects wrought by nature.

Reply. The argument would be valid if God *needed* the coöperation of creatures in order to achieve the results. But on any reasonable theory of creation, the participation of creatures is a largess of the Creator. Moreover, the evident aptitude of the creature [8] would be futile, and would argue unwisdom if not deception on the part of the Creator.

3. In any case, God must be admitted as a partial cause. But it is unbecoming that the Creator should be a partner with the creature in producing the effect.

Reply. The two causes are of essentially different orders. God sustains the creature in existence both as idle and as active. Thus the very existence of the creature's substance, its powers and its actions are due to the constant efficiency of the divine omnipotence. No such causality can be ascribed to the creature.

Action at a Distance

In this phrase, "distance" has a technical meaning. It means that the two bodies in question are not only not in contact, but are separated by an absolute vacuum, that they are totally isolated from one another, without any communicating medium whatsoever—or at least without any medium which is at all capable of communicating a particular given force. The locomotive pulls the observation coach at a distance, but the train serves as an apt medium for the traction. The classic problem is: Can a body completely surrounded by a total vacuum [9] act upon a body "at a distance" in that sense. The Dynamists answer most emphatically, Yes. They

---

[8] E.g., of the eye.
[9] I.e., a vacuum not only void of air but of ether as well.

hold that no action ever takes place or can take place except at a distance. Other physicists answer, No. Since the testimony of these physicists is based upon reasonable induction, and not on *a priori* theories, it seems sufficient to establish the physical impossibility of "action at a distance." Whether it be metaphysically impossible, is more difficult to decide, and must be left to the abstract discussion of the categories of *actio et passio*. Still, when we speak of contact as being physically necessary for interaction between material substances, it must not be thought that we postulate the actual contact of ponderable matter. As far as is known, two particles of ponderable matter cannot be brought into such contact by any power at our command. Two molecules cohere with great force without at the same time having their ponderable parts in contact. Their resistance to such contact is too great for us to overcome. For all that, we do not suppose that this resistance exists across a vacuum; physicists insist that there is imponderable matter between the ponderable parts.

Qualities of Bodies

Quantity, i.e., extension, is a static property of bodies. It is sometimes called an "attribute" to indicate that it is a characteristic of all bodily substance. Qualities, on the other hand, are active properties, and vary with different substances. Some qualities are more or less stable in a given substance; for example, color, odor, taste; and these are termed "specific properties." Other qualities may come and go without any substantial difference in the subject. Examples of this kind are motion, temperature, electric charge. They are usually described as "conditions." We do not wish here to make any distinction between stable and variable qualities, but shall treat them indiscriminately.

The ancients recognized four primitive qualities: hot, cold, dry and moist; secondary qualities were such as made a substance heavy or light, hard or soft, viscous or brittle, rough or smooth, dense or rarefied. Modern physics has advanced far beyond this elementary classification of qualities, and experimental psychology has discovered many things about our perception of qualities. In order to get an understanding of what qualities mean, we must first distinguish between the perception of qualities, and the qualities themselves as they exist in the body independently of their being perceived. The former contains problems for epistemology and psychology to solve, the latter alone falls within the scope of cosmology. It is necessary, therefore, for clearness' sake to preserve a distinct line of demarcation between the ontological properties of bodies on the one hand, and on the other our subjective psychological reaction to them as well as our certainty of their existence and differences. Let us illustrate with color. Color, ontologically, is a definite potency of a body to absorb certain wave-lengths of light and reject others. That potency exists even when the body is in complete darkness. When light falls upon it that potency is actuated; the actual operation of handling the light in a particular way, whether or not an eye be aware of it, is the body's ontological or "physical" color. In such sense we mean to deal with properties here.

At the same time we do not wish to call in question the certainty of our sense perceptions; and hence do not recognize Locke's division of "primary" and "secondary" qualities. For Locke the "primary" qualities were such as directly involve quantity, as bulk, shape and motion.[10] He held that only the "primary" qualities had real existence in the object. He denied such reality to the "secondary" qualities—color, taste, etc.; and he did so for the simple reason that he failed to recognize the difference between the ontological property itself and our psychological reaction to it. Now, we hold that there are differences in the external objects which account for the differences in our sense-experience with regard to them. By this we do not mean that we can perceive *all* the different characteristics of an object; there are factors revealed to the sensitized plate, by ultra-violet rays and X-rays, which our senses cannot of themselves discern. Nor is it meant that each of us has the same psychological experience in regard to an identical object. We will not instance the case of the color-blind person, for he merely fails to see differences which others are aware of; just as some of the brute animals may perceive differences of color which to man are impossible of perception. But even between two persons of normal vision one may experience a more vivid reaction than the other with respect to the identical object. Nor is it impossible that, if they

---

[10] By motion he means that which is perceptible as motion; not, therefore, heat or sound, but, e.g., a swinging pendulum.

could exchange or compare their subjective experiences, one might call red what the other had been accustomed to call green. Admitting all that, we still hold that there are differences of some kind in objects which tally with the differences in my reaction to them.

Before animals appeared on the face of the earth, there were without doubt many sounds in nature, the booming of the waves, the crash of the thunder, the roar of the avalanche; and yet not an ear extant to hear these sounds. Can it be said that there was sound then? A great discussion has raged around this point. Is sound nothing else than the resonant object? Or is it in the reverberating air? Or in the excited end-organs of hearing? Or in the brain? The disputants do not differ about the data. They wish to decide which item has the best right to be called sound "formally," leaving the rest to fill the rôle of sound "fundamentally" or "causally." Some of the physical and physiological factors have been enumerated in the interrogations above. But most writers will not admit that it is sound *par excellence* until it has become psychic, conscious, and is referred back to the object which originated the stimulus. Similar replies are given in regard to color and other properties.

In cosmology we leave out the physiological and psychical reactions to the qualities of bodies, and confine ourselves to qualities considered physically. Thus we can say that physical color is formally in the external object; so also is physical sound, etc. What, then, are physical qualities? Some are directly recognizable by the senses. These are colors, sounds, savors, odors, temperatures and resistance, the last named including hardness, softness, smoothness, roughness, weight, mass, etc. Color as a physical property of a body is the body's capacity to reflect certain kinds of light; and the body is denominated red, blue, etc., not according to the light which it absorbs, but according to that which it rejects. Sound is a particular kind of vibration which may be taken up by the air and carried to the ear. A body's sound depends ultimately on its structure, and proximately on the condition in which it is. Ontologically the sound is this peculiar type of vibration, and may exist in a vacuum. Savor, or taste, is, like odor, usually considered a chemical property. Temperature is a degree of molecular agitation. Resistance in its various phases is due to properties difficult to identify. In general, we can say that in gases the molecules are detached from one another, in liquids moderately attached, and in crystals or solids firmly attached; and that, similarly, the qualities enumerated under resistance, except weight and mass, are basically molecular states. Weight is the capacity of a body to respond to the gravitational attraction of another body. Mass is an absolute property, independent of the proximity of other bodies, whereby a body resists a change in its state of motion or rest. Science is as yet unable to point out the exact nature of weight and mass.

Some qualities of bodies are not recognizable except in an extended field. Thus the qualities associated with perceptible motion, whether that motion be a change within the compass of the body itself, or relative to other bodies, need a background which is extended. All sensible qualities must, of course, be extended, but they do not all need reference to other extension as is the case with motion. Mere figure or shape is not a quality; for though it is not perceptible to us except by the active properties of color and resistance, it is in itself merely a determination of extension. Lastly, there are properties which are in no way directly arrived at by sensation, but only by inference from sensation: these are magnetism, electrical charge, chemical affinity, and many other forces dealt with in the natural sciences. And it is to these sciences that we must leave the description of the physical character of such qualities.

The Kinetic Theory of Qualities

As we have touched on this subject in the prenotes to the preceding thesis, very little comment is needed here. A strict kinetic theory of qualities must maintain that all qualities are ontologically nothing else than matter in motion. This is not the same as saying that all qualities are accompanied with motion, or give rise to motion. Against the kinetic theory we hold that (1) there is some inner reason why even the smallest particles of matter move *in a certain way,* and (2) that there are many phenomena which cannot be explained by supposing bodies to be merely striking against one another after the manner of molecules in a gas. As regards the first point, the smallest particles of matter known are electrons and protons, and the mere mention of them is sufficient to show that their manner of action

is determined by some intrinsic principle, that they
are endowed with some force which holds them
to their characteristic activities. The same is true
of the atoms and the molecules in respect to their
specific properties. Activities there are, and these
are accompanied with motion; but these activities
could never hold their specific character unless they
were *controlled from within*. Our opponents [11] cannot logically maintain this control from within, and
therefore, however much they may strive to avoid
the predicament, are forced by their theory to resort
to the mere impact of particles. On this second
point we object that the resultants of impact are
indefinitely variable, and hence should never produce the fixed and invariable properties which occur
in millions of instances in bodies even too small to
be seen by the naked eye, not to speak of their consistency throughout all nature. Moreover the very
particles must have cohesion, otherwise no impact
is possible. To attempt to explain all the phenomena of nature by repulsion alone without attraction, adhesion or selective action, is plainly futile
at the very outset.

Topics for Discussion. Occasionalism. The
ancient physical theory of the influence of the
heavens in communicating efficiency to the lower
spheres. Is action at a distance metaphysically impossible? Activity in the ether. Was there sound
on earth previous to the advent of animals capable
of hearing? Physical and psychological color,
sound, etc.

[11] E.g., Stallo, Chwolson, Dressel.

REFERENCES

Cath. Ency. "Cause." "Quality."

Coffey, P. *Epistemology,* Vol. 1.

Gruender, H. *Experimental Psychology,* Ch. 14.

Nys, D. In *Manual of Modern Scholastic Philosophy,* Vol. 1, Ch. 2, art. 4.

O'Neill, J. *Cosmology,* Vol. 1, Ch. 8.

CHAPTER XIII

THE ADEQUATE CONCEPT OF PHYSICAL LAWS

SCOPE OF THE THESIS. The term "natural bodies" includes all objects as they occur in nature without interference on the part of man. It excludes man-made contrivances of all kinds, machines, houses, roadways, engineering achievements, etc. These latter are by philosophers called "artificial bodies"; and although the laws of nature are by no means annulled in these constructions, still the forces of nature are arbitrarily rearranged at the discretion of the human builder or manipulator. It is for the sake of clearness, then, that we leave out of consideration any but natural bodies. Secondly, by the term "natural bodies" we wish to exclude all beings possessed of intelligence. Thus we rule out all *human acts.* These acts are indeed governed by law, but a different kind of law from that with which we are dealing here. The deliberate acts of man, not only when they are confined to his spiritual nature, but even when they involve outward bodily activity, are outside the state of the question in this thesis. We do not, however, mean to restrict our considerations to inorganic nature alone. As in the thesis on finality, so also here we may permit excursions of our thought into the *vegetative and animal realms,* and should be justified in illustrating our subject from the sense and vegetal life of man in those operations, such as digestion and the functioning of the nerves, which are not directly the outcome of the individual's free choice.

WHAT IS LAW? "A law," says St. Thomas, "is a rational ordinance for the common good, promulgated by the one who has charge of the community." [1] Good is mentioned as the purpose of law; reason is required to apprehend the good, and to decide upon the means to attain it; law is therefore called an ordinance of reason. But a law must be promulgated, the regulation decided upon must be communicated to the subjects. In the case of rational subjects the ordinance is promulgated by being *made known* to them. In the case of irrational subjects it cannot as such be made known to them; hence to irrational beings the regulation is communicated by imparting to them a definite inclination, or "bent" of their nature. We see this inclination, this nisus, in the instincts of animals, to seek food, to avoid danger, etc. We see it in the operation of breathing, in the way the heart is set upon its task, and in all the functions of vegetative and sense life. We see it in the fixed activities of all the inorganic elements and compounds. And it must be noted that the immediate directive force in these operations is within the agent; natural objects are not pushed about by some external force as "men" on a chess-board; they perform the feats themselves by their innate tendencies to act and react in certain definite ways. In order, however, that these actions be due to law it is not enough that they

[1] *Sum. th.* I, II, q.90, a.4.

proceed from an interior principle. The source of the action and of the kind of action must indeed be within the immediate agent; the agent itself must possess the inclination or "bent." But to have law the inclination must have been *put there* by the Supreme Power. For it is by the act of *imparting* inclinations to these beings that the law is "promulgated" to them. The aptitude and inclination are not only possessed, they are *given*—for the purposes intended by the Giver or Lawmaker. Law, therefore, is not an external norm; it is an internal, imparted norm.

DIVISIONS OF LAW. We may now define "physical law" as *the fixed inclination with which irrational beings are endowed for the regulation of natural events*. Law is said to be *"actively"* in the legislator, *"passively"* in the subjects it is imposed upon, and *"effectively"* in the ordered events which result from the law. *Moral* law is that imposed upon intelligent and free beings for the regulation of their deliberate acts. Even in this case, however, there is a basic inclination implanted in the being's nature, and it consists in the love of the good and the desire of happiness. All law, physical or moral, is a part of, or a participation in, the *eternal law* by which the Divine Wisdom determines for all creatures, existing and possible, their proper ends and the appropriate means for attaining those ends. A law is *natural* if it is as such contained in the being's nature, it is a *positive* law if it concerns matters left undermined by nature but in accordance with it. Positive laws [2] have reference only to the natural

[2] E.g., civil and ecclesiastic legislation.

moral law, and are supplementary to it. Even God's decrees in appointing a supernatural destiny for man, and in establishing the Church, are positive divine laws; for they are in no way contained in nature, though they are in accord with it. In the realm of irrational creatures there is only natural law, there are no positive laws for them. All the actions of irrational beings are dictated by their natures in response to their surroundings.

VARIATIONS OF THE TERM "LAW." Given certain fixed conditions, there is uniformity in the activity of natural bodies. The sciences of physics and chemistry, and all the other natural sciences are built upon the recognition of this uniformity, and in our practical life we continually depend upon it. We use wax for candles but not for furnaces, we drink water but not vitriol; because we know the way these things act, and do not expect them to change their methods. When we call this uniformity of action "law," we are not using the term "law" in the sense in which it is employed in our thesis. *Uniformity* of activity is not in itself a law, it is the *effect* of law. Again the expression or *statement* of this uniformity, whether the expression be oral, or written or in mathematical symbols, is sometimes called a "law," e.g., $M=mv$. To avoid such meanings of "law" we have used the term "genuine law." A genuine law includes in its concept a superior and a subject; a genuine law is *imposed*. For that reason we say that natural objects are *endowed* with certain tendencies. This is what we mean to prove in our argument. The uniformity of activity is accepted as a fact, it is not in dispute.

The proper expression of this uniformity we leave to the experts in the various sciences. The notion of law which we wish to establish is that which includes a lawgiver. That concept of law is not adverted to in the particular sciences, but it is not excluded by their data; on the contrary, these data are precisely our ground for asserting the fact of genuine physical laws. If we advance beyond the point at which the sciences stop, that is only because philosophy should have no justification if it contributed to our knowledge nothing more than is contributed by the restricted natural sciences. Philosophy, too, is a natural science, but it is not restrained in its conclusions to certain prescribed fields; it may draw any conclusion for which the premises are discovered in nature.

ORDER AND COURSE OF NATURE. By the *course of nature* is understood the sequence of events. The *order of nature* is the local arrangement in which the various bodies in the universe are placed with respect to one another at any given moment. The original order of nature must be ascribed to the Creator; the subsequent orders of nature, except where interfered with by the arbitrary intervention of man or of God, are due to the workings of the necessarily acting natural forces.

OPPONENTS. The adversaries to this thesis are the same as those who oppose finality,[3] Epicurus, Democritus, atheistic Evolutionists, Materialists, Naturalists who identify evolving nature with an evolving god,[4] and Pantheists generally. *We agree*

[3] Cf. Th. 2.
[4] E.g., Alexander, Whitehead, etc.

with our opponents that *matter acts from internal
necessity;* but to stop there is to leave the entire
philosophical question unanswered, and to declare
philosophy bankrupt. Our opponents, as Aristotle
said of Democritus, have "lazily neglected" to push
their inquiry further.[5]

*Thesis 13. The activities of natural bodies are
governed by genuine laws*

Argument. A genuine law is a regulation (1)
emanating from intelligence, (2) looking to the
common good, and (3) imposed by the one in
charge. But the activities of natural bodies are
governed by such regulation. Therefore the activities of natural bodies are governed by genuine laws.

The major is the definition of law explained
above. It need only be remarked that the promulgation, or communication, of a law carries with it
the *sanction,* that is the *necessity* of conforming.

The minor. (1) It is abundantly clear that the
activities of the material world are highly rational.
The instincts of animals, the processes of sensation
and vegetation, the physical and chemical operations
whether on a grand or a minute scale, fill the mind
of man with wonder at the intelligence displayed.

(2) Although each thing, given the external conditions, must react, and do so in a specified way,
still it attains its own particular end, or, failing that,
contributes to the promotion of the good of some
other being. Hence the rule of nature is for the
common good.

(3) Since material beings have no intelligence of

[5] *Metaph.* I. 4.

their own,[6] it follows that the intelligence they display in their activities is not their own. The case is parallel to that of a machine which displays the intelligence of the maker. In other words, natural bodies act according to a plan that is highly rational; this plan cannot be ascribed to them; it is the plan of someone else. Secondly, they act according to that plan by internal necessity, as is admitted by all; hence the plan is implanted in their very natures. Therefore it is imposed by the One Who has supreme charge of the material world.

In this way only can the activities of matter be reasonably understood, namely, that they are governed by genuine laws.

Difficulties. 1. Law requires an intelligent subject.

Reply. A moral or ethical law requires such a subject, but a physical law does not. Each thing must be directed according to its nature; a free being by a manifestion of the decree to the understanding, by the will's desire for well-being, and by the sanction of the law; a non-free being by the nisus of its nature always to act, given the conditions, and to act in a specified way.

2. The being's nature is the reason for its manner of acting; therefore it is a law unto itself.

Reply. The being's nature is the *immediate* reason, I grant. The being's nature can be the *ultimate* reason, I deny.

3. The constancy of the activities of nature can never be demonstrated, for "if some one were to assert that from to-day on, night is not going to follow day nor death follow life, nobody could refute him." [7]

[6] Or even if they had as much as man, could never succeed in maintaining such uniformity and coöperation.
[7] Becher.

Reply. Whatever may be the constancy of activity in the future, there has been sufficient constancy in the past to justify our assertion that it is due to nature.

4. Though there may be constancy in nature we can never really know it; for we depend after all on our instruments of measurements, which are never absolutely accurate, and there are so many and such minute forces entering into every test that it is hopeless to take account of them all; the whole process gives us only average results of forces that may be acting with no uniformity at all.

Reply. If this objection were in the main true it must surely shake the foundations of all the natural sciences. For ordinary cases it can be rejected *in toto.* If, however, we wish our measurements to be extremely accurate, e.g., in the conservation of energy throughout the changes of matter from the non-living to the living matter, it must be admitted that we cannot with any great certainty assert that absolutely not the slightest quantity of new energy has appeared. However, in order to speak correctly of laws of nature we need not know for certain that there is not even a hairline divergence from uniformity. On the other hand if we wish to set down definitions of physical laws which cannot be quarreled with, we find that difficult—not from the lack of very obvious uniformity,[8] but because when the law is applied on a very minute scale, factors may enter which were negligible on a larger scale. This, nevertheless, does *not in the least infringe* upon the universality and uniformity of the law as applied on the larger scale. The uniformity *there* is absolute.

Topics for Discussion. Difference between natural moral law and natural physical law. The "promulgation" of the law in the mineral, vegetative, sentient and rational realms. Law of the

[8] As for instance in the law of gravity.

"path of least resistance," or least expenditure of energy.

REFERENCES

Nys, D. In *Manual of Modern Scholastic Philosophy,* Vol. 1, Ch. 4.
Windle, B. *The Church and Science,* Ch. 13.

CHAPTER XIV

MORAL, PHYSICAL AND ABSOLUTE NECESSITY. A thing is necessary if it could not be otherwise than it is. Thus the sum of two and three is necessarily five, for it could not be otherwise. But necessity is of three kinds. When we say *cannot,* we may mean cannot in any one of three senses. If a candidate for office says that he cannot get everybody in the country to vote for him, he means that it is, for him at least, *morally impossible.* A "moral impossibility" is whatever is beyond the power of the human will to achieve. It is a moral impossibility for us to live our entire lives without committing the slightest fault. A thing is *physically impossible* if it cannot be done by the natural forces employed. An ocean liner cannot be moored with a rope of water, the tides cannot be turned back by word of mouth, as King Canute was at pains to show. A thing is *metaphysically impossible* if it cannot be effected by any means whatever, not even by the omnipotence of God. Accordingly, if it is morally impossible for a thing to be otherwise, then it is *morally necessary;* if physically impossible, then it is *physically necessary;* if it is metaphysically impossible for it to be otherwise, then it is a case of metaphysical, or *absolute necessity.* It is this last named necessity which we deny exists in the physical laws.

HYPOTHETICAL NECESSITY. There is no question in our thesis about moral necessity; the dispute is whether the forces of nature act with absolute necessity, or only physical necessity. Metaphysical necessity is called absolute because it is unconditioned. Thus we say that the existence and the attributes of God are absolutely necessary because they are independent of any condition whatever. *Absolute necessity* is therefore that which is independent of any condition or proviso. On the other hand, the material world and its forces do not necessarily exist, their existence is contingent on the will of the Creator, and their non-existence is readily conceivable. But even granted their existence, it must also be granted that the forces of nature can be annulled, overcome or supplanted by the Power that made them. Hence the necessity with which material agents act is conditioned on the non-interference of the Maker. Such necessity is called hypothetical. *Hypothetical necessity* is therefore that which is dependent upon some condition which need not be verified. Now, our purpose here is not to show that the course of nature is necessary, that is beyond dispute; we intend, however, to show that the necessity is hypothetical, and not absolute.

MATERIAL CONDITIONS ESSENTIAL TO PHYSICAL NECESSITY. It is needful for clearness' sake to name definitely what conditions we are speaking of. When we say that the activity of material agents is dependent on conditions, we *do not mean* by conditions the *material surroundings* of the agent. Surely for fire to burn there must be inflammable material and available oxygen. Without the requisite conditions of matter physical agents will not act. There is no necessity whatever unless these material conditions are present. To predicate any necessity of nature is to suppose the material requisites to be at hand. The statement of a physical law includes them; and we say that, granted all these material requisites, the force cannot but act and act in a certain way. We do not wish to impugn that necessity; we suppose it; it is about that necessity we are speaking when we say it is a hypothetical necessity. This natural necessity thus understood is the subject of our proposition; the predicate is the negative "not absolute."

NECESSITY IN THE SEQUENCE OF EVENTS. We have seen that a physical law as it exists in the natural body is a fixed tendency under certain material conditions to produce a definite effect. The fixed tendency together with the requisite conditions is called the law in the first period, stage or act; the resulting effect, the event, is the law in the second act. Now, what we say in our thesis is that the event does not follow with absolute necessity. Events make up the course of nature; their sequence is necessary, but only physically so. Evidently we are not concerned with anything but the resulting effect, and we say that God can prevent that effect from occurring. Man, too, can prevent natural events from happening, as when he builds a dike to keep out the sea; man is as a matter of fact constantly changing the course of nature: but man does so by arbitrarily playing one natural force against another; he freely makes use of the necessarily act-ing forces; he changes the material conditions, but granted a certain set of conditions he cannot prevent the event from happening. All this merely means that man cannot in the technical sense overcome physical necessity. But we cannot deny to God the power, with all the requisite material conditions present, to prevent the natural effect from taking place, or to produce a different effect, thus *suspend-ing the necessity* which rules the events of the material world. In doing so He need not abrogate the law which is expressed in the nature of the mate-rial agents concerned; for the tendencies may still remain, though void of their proper effect.

ADVERSARIES. The opponents of the thesis may be classified as *Materialists,* who hold absolute deter-minism in the processes of nature, and deny that there is anything extant except matter; and *Panthe-ists,* whose dogma it is that the one only being evolves with absolute necessity.

Thesis 14. The necessity which rules the events of the material world is not absolute

Argument. The necessity which rules the events of the material world is only physical, that is, it is hypothetical and not absolute, if, granted all the material conditions requisite for the event to occur, its occurrence is still contingent on the power of the Creator. But such is the case. Therefore . . .

The major. The only necessity which is beyond the power of God to set aside is metaphysical or abso-lute necessity. If, therefore, the necessity with which material forces act can be annulled by omnipotence, it is only hypothetical necessity. It must be noted, however, that the major does not deny that these forces act with necessity; nor does the minor deny that; both premises suppose real physical necessity.

The minor. (a) No creature can act without the *concurrent power* of God; and God is not bound to give that concurrence. If He were bound He would be subject to the creature He had made. But any dependence of God on a work of His own hands must be destructive of the whole nature of God, Who is supremely independent of anything distinct from himself. (b) The Creator, Who without employing any material force [1] originally produced the forces of nature, can, without employing any such force, *impede* the action of the forces in existence, *heighten* or *lessen* their power, or *divert* them to other than their connatural objects. All this God can do without undoing the nature of the material agents. Lastly, it is sufficient that omnipotence *can* so affect the course of nature; that course remains only physically necessary even if God should never exercise His dominion over it.

Difficulties. 1. Science demonstrates that there are no possible exceptions to the laws of nature.

Reply. That there are no exceptions physically possible, I grant. That exceptions are metaphysically impossible, I deny. Physically science does not concern itself about the metaphysical possibility of exceptions to the physical laws.

2. The physical laws emanate from the very nature of matter; to thwart the law is to destroy the nature.

Reply. The physical laws understood as the innate ten-

[1] For none previously existed.

dencies of matter do emanate from, or may be said to constitute, the nature of the matter in question; but those tendencies may remain even when the effect is not forthcoming. Man may alter the course of nature which has been predetermined by irrational forces, and do so arbitrarily. In this respect man's interference does not differ from God's. In either case the necessary course of nature is set aside. The difference lies in the fact that man employs material forces, while God produces the result without resorting to the use of material forces. But in both cases the nature of the matter involved remains intact.

3. Essences are eternal and necessary; therefore, they are in no sense hypothetical.

Reply. The essences, even of material things, are eternal and necessary, if by essence you mean the mere compatibility of notes, i.e., the abstract objective possibility; but they are not eternal and necessary if you mean the *existing* essence, for they are contingent beings, and therefore their existence is hypothetical. And, granting their existence as fixed, their essence is not destroyed, when they fail to produce the event which they have the innate tendency to produce, no more than a stone held aloft in the hand loses its essence because it does not fall.

Topics for Discussion. Is there genuine law in Spinoza's pantheism? Can man break the physical laws? How man changes the course of nature.

REFERENCES

Cath. Ency. "Necessity." "Contingency." "Nature."
Month, Vol. 104, p. 20. "Gospel of the Non-miraculous."
Shallo, M. *Scholastic Philosophy,* "Cosmology."

CHAPTER XV

THE POSSIBILITY OF MIRACLES

DEFINITION OF MIRACLE. A miracle is a perceptible event, forming an exception to the course of nature and effected by divine intervention. The word "miracle" comes from *mirari,* to wonder at, and is often used in a broad sense to denote anything that causes wonderment. The above definition is a technical one, determining the sense in which we propose to defend miracles in this thesis. We say that a miracle is *"perceptible,"* by which we mean that it is an *object of sense perception.* Hence, the infusion of grace into the soul, the mystery of transubstantiation, etc., are not miracles in our sense, for they are not perceptible to the faculties of sensation. We say that a miracle is *"an exception to the course of nature"* in order to signify that under the given circumstances the natural *forces of themselves called for some other event* than the one which happened. According to this the creation of the human soul is not a miracle, and should not be even were it a directly perceptible effect, because the creation of the soul is called for by the forces of nature; though those forces cannot of themselves produce a soul. It is not an exception to the course of nature, but the necessary complement to the natural forces whereby the course of nature is fulfilled. And although this is a case of direct divine intervention, it is ruled out of the category of miracles for the reason stated.[1] When, therefore, we say that a miracle is *"effected by divine intervention,"* we wish further to restrict the concept of exception. In our definition, then, the remote genus is "perceptible event," the proximate genus is "exception," and the ultimate specific difference is "effected by divine intervention." This last differentiating note is necessary, because, as we have seen, man may within a limited sphere interfere with the course of nature at will. The products of human art, from the stone hatchet to the radio, are witnesses to man's power to intervene in nature. For this reason we say there is no miracle unless there is intervention on the part of God. We have already noted the difference between the way in which God intervenes and the way in which man does. A further discussion of this point must be left to the next thesis, but it is necessary here to specify what we understand by the term "divine," in our definition. By this term we mean to state that the *immediate source* of the intervention is *outside the material universe,* and that the *ultimate, principal cause* of the fact of intervention is none other than the *Creator Himself.*

THE POSSIBILITY OF INTERVENTION BY CREATED SPIRITS. In philosophy we do not positively know

[1] For the same reason the first appearance of plant life and animal life on earth, though they too required divine intervention, may be disqualified as miracles in our technical meaning; for in the readiness of matter for the appearance of those forms of life at the given periods, and in the plan of the Creator that His work should culminate in man, there was a certain natural call for the origin and development of the lesser species.

of the existence of created pure spirits, or angels. We know at best that such beings are possible. The only pure spirit to Whose *existence* we can conclude from the natural evidence of the universe is God. But since we know that the human soul is a spirit, though not a pure spirit as it is united in one supposit with the body, it is clearly possible that there should be other created spirits that are not destined for union with matter. Hence, we must reckon at least on the *possibility of such spirits*. And what their power over the forces of matter may be is a thing which is difficult for us to know. We know that the human soul has sway over the material forces of the body. Hence it is quite likely that angels may be able to do at least as much, even though they do not form supposits with the matter they have sway over. We have made allowance for this contingency in our interpretation of the definition of a miracle; for in any case the created spirits are under the dominion of the Creator, which leaves to Him the rôle of principal cause. For all we know an angel may be able by its own power to effect the kind of intervention described in our definition; but in that case the angel certainly cannot act without the authorization of the Creator, and thereby becomes His *"moral instrument"* in producing the effect. If the angel cannot serve even in that capacity, then God must perform the miracle directly Himself. In any case, God is ultimately the principal cause.

DIVISION OF MIRACLES. Miracles are usually divided into three classes according as the substance, the manner, or the subject of the effect exceeds the power of nature. The *"substance"* of the event is beyond nature, when nature simply cannot produce the effect at all, given any amount of opportunity, as the conversion of water into wine by a word. The miracle is one of *manner* when nature can produce the effect, but not in that way; as the sudden cessation of the waves of the sea. The third kind is had when nature can produce the effect, but not in the given *subject;* as restoring life to a dead body.

RELATION OF THE THESIS TO THE PRECEDING. The present thesis is not identical with the preceding one, and that for two reasons: (1) In the preceding thesis we determined that the necessity of nature's activity is hypothetical by the very fact of the creature's intrinsic and direct dependence on the dominion of the Creator; the necessity remains hypothetical even if God never exercised His power to intervene.[2] In the present thesis we consider whether there are any reasons *within the Creator Himself* why He should not exercise that power. (2) The power which can work a miracle is not narrowed down by our definition to the unique and absolute dominion of God. We admit the possibility of participation in the effect by other agents less than God, though superior to man. An angel may be able to manipulate the forces of nature arbitrarily, as man does, and in a way entirely superior to the efficiency of which man is capable. All this means an exception to the necessary course of nature, but it is effected by the *free* employment of the forces already extant. For we are ready to admit with the scientists that the energy used by man both in the activities of his own body and in the influence he exerts on the material things about him is not new energy, but is the extant energy of matter under a new control, and a free control. The same manipulation of

[2] The corresponding potency on the part of the creature is called "obediential," and can be evoked by none but the Creator.

energy may be possible to the created pure spirits; and we admit such an agency in the case of miracles. The exercise of this power is not a proof that the necessity of nature's course is hypothetical in the sense defended in the previous thesis.

OPPONENTS OF THE THESIS. Adversaries to the thesis are the *Atheists,* who besides denying the existence of God, usually also deny the existence of pure spirits, or at least their interference in the material world; *Pantheists* and *Materialists,* who recognize only absolute necessity in the processes of nature; the *Deists,* who while they admit an extramundane and spiritual Deity, maintain that He exercises no providence over the world, but leaves it entirely to itself to work out its own destiny; and the *Rationalists,* who consider it would argue an imperfection in God if He interfered in the course of nature. Among all these it is the "accepted thing" to suppose the impossibility of miracles, and to criticize history and the Scriptures according to that fundamental dogma. Individual writers are Renan, D. F. Strauss, Haeckel, Harnack, B. Bauer, Spinoza, etc.

Thesis 15. Miracles are possible

Argument 1. Miracles are possible if there is nothing on the part of the physical laws or on the part of God to render them impossible. But on neither account is there anything to render them impossible. Therefore miracles are possible.

The minor. (1) The physical laws are (a) only hypothetically necessary, as was shown in the preceding thesis, and hence cannot be an obstacle to intervention by the Creator. The physical laws (b) do not prevent arbitrary interference by man, and consequently it is irrational to suppose that God or even a created spirit could not make the forces of nature produce effects which could never have occurred had the forces been left to themselves.

(2) There is nothing on the part of God Himself to prevent His freely interfering with the course of nature. The two attributes concerned, as the opponents admit, are His immutability and His wisdom. But His *immutability* does not prevent Him from making exceptions to the course of nature; for God need not, and cannot, be supposed to decree the law first, and then to decide upon an exception, but He decrees the two together. Nor is this against His *wisdom;* for it is not to be thought that God has recourse to miracles in order to correct His own laws. He could attain all the natural ends of the physical order without once interfering in the operations of nature. When He interferes He does so for a higher good, a moral good; to authorize some teaching as coming from Him and having His sanction, to express His love or His warning in a striking and personal manner. Now he cannot attain this effect unless by some sign which mere nature cannot produce; in other words, the event cannot be a means to *this* end unless it be an *exception* to the necessary course of nature. Therefore, instead of correcting His handiwork, God is making it serve a higher purpose.

Argument 2. God must be able to speak directly

to men; but He cannot do so unless miracles are possible: therefore miracles are possible.

The minor. In order to communicate with men God must give men a sign by which they can know for certain that the message comes from Him, and the sign best qualified for that purpose is a miracle. (Even a direct illumination of the mind cannot, of itself, carry the authority of God, unless the illumination have the character of a miracle.)

Argument 3. Miracles are possible, if they have occurred; but they have occurred, as anyone of unprejudiced mind may discover for himself by honest and thorough investigation. In our own times we need only instance the case of Lourdes.

Difficulties.   1. Should God permit miracles He would destroy the security necessary for ordered human existence, for that security is based on the necessary operation of the physical laws.

Reply. If exceptions to the necessary course of nature became so *frequent* as to be the rule, and occurred without any *premonition,* and without our being able at the time to *distinguish* them from the course of nature, they would indeed disturb the even tenor of our lives. But the possibility of miracles does not mean all this; in fact, such conditions would rob them of their very purpose for being performed at all. Unless they are infrequent they must lose much of their power to compel attention; if they are to serve as a sign they must usually be appealed to beforehand, and thus their occurrence does not disturb our security; in order to engender certainty they must be recognizable as exceptions, and a recognized exception does not infringe the certainty which is based on the law. We are, as a matter of fact, constantly experiencing variations from the necessary course of nature. It is an exception to that necessary course for iron, rubber and gasoline to come together in the form of a motor car and go faring about the world at the caprice of man; and though these antics of matter may disturb our sense of security, they in no way destroy our faith in what nature will do if left to itself and allowed to pursue its own course. So, too, even if miracles happened frequently and we recognized them as *free interferences* from outside the visible universe, we need not be upset so long as we knew the interference was under *benign control:* such control is included in the very possibility of miracles. Lastly, the necessarily acting forces more often take us by surprise than miracles are supposed to do; for example, earthquakes, storms, explosions of power magazines, etc. These things occur by the necessary forces of nature, but we are not sufficiently acquainted with the forces and the conditions to know what to expect or when it may happen. By such puerile objections do the Rationalists seek to impugn the possibility of miracles.

2. Science accepts the principle of "closed causality," namely that nothing happens in the world except by forces already extant within the world. But this excludes intervention from outside.

Reply. (a) Science has not proved such to be the case by complete induction, and can scarcely ever hope to do so. (b) Even supposing the principle to be true, it does not exclude miracles; for first of all both God and created spirits may in a given case do nothing more than employ the forces already extant, just as man does, and secondly if God wishes to exercise His absolute dominion, He may bring about the exceptional effect by merely holding certain forces in check (which He does without the consumption of material energy) while letting others have sway naturally. Not even the law of the conservation of energy is disturbed. Still, exceptions certainly can be made outright by the Creator in the case of any physical law.

3. God may either will or not will the law; but according to the thesis He does both at once, for He lets the tendencies, with all the material conditions requisite for action, remain inoperative.

Reply. There is no contradiction in allowing the material agent to retain its nature, and at the same time suspend the effect. And since God wills both from the very beginning, He cannot be said to be mutable in His counsels. Likewise, if He wishes to vary the natural effect by reinforcing the power of one agent and diminishing that of another, He may do so without even infringing the law of the conservation of energy, for surely He Who created the world's energy may transfer and transform it at will.

4. God, if He wrought a miracle, would be correcting His own handiwork.

Reply. The objection supposes that miracles are resorted to for the sake of the mere physical good resulting from them. No advocate of the possibility of miracles has ever maintained that; for God could, e.g., see to it that a man were cured by purely natural means, or by the same means prevent him from falling sick. The value of a miracle as such lies in the fact that it is an *exception*. Besides, there is not utter rigidity in the course of nature, as though nature were a resistless machine. Man never ceases to modify the course of nature; and the working out of God's providence through freely operating human wills, and in spite of them, is much more a marvel than physical miracles.

5. God cannot change the moral law, therefore He cannot change the physical law.

Reply. There is an essential difference between the natural moral law and the natural physical law. The former, in its basic principles, has a direct and necessary connection with the *final purpose of creation,* which is the formal glory of God, or, under another aspect, the complete and lasting happiness of His rational creatures. Therefore, for God to

release man from the moral law were identical with giving
up the final purpose of creation and abandoning the whole
plan.   But irrational creatures do not stand in that same
direct relation to the final purpose, hence their law need
not be invariable.   Moreover, as we have seen, the physical
law is not necessarily abrogated in miracles.   The effects
which must occur if the forces are left to themselves are
thwarted, and other results produced; the law remains intact.
If this interference is by man it is a human work; if it is
done by an extramundane power, with the direct approval
of God, it is a miracle.

The Purpose of Miracles

Granted that God is omnipotent and omniscient,
the purpose of miracles is not to secure a material
good.   The purpose of miracles is to secure some
moral good; and that moral good is of a particular
kind and to be secured in a particular way.   The
necessary forces of nature left to themselves or
manipulated by man are sufficient to express the
existence and bounty of the Creator.   But if God
desires to make known to man the free decrees of
His will, over and above those to which He has
committed Himself by the fact of creation, He must
employ some other means than those offered by the
necessarily acting forces of nature.   These free
choices of God cannot be known to us unless God
speaks to us, unless He tell us Himself that which
nature cannot tell.   In order that we may know
it is God Who vouches for the truth of the communication, some sign must be given us.   That sign
is the miracle; it is God's seal of approval.   Thus
man's elevation to a supernatural destiny could never

be known from the study of nature alone. The free decree of God can be known only on the authority of God revealing it. We believe on the authority of God, indeed; but we need the sign to let us know it is God Who speaks. God may also use a miracle to express His providence in a special manner, e.g., by the cure of a sick person in answer to prayer. These moral values are in no way attainable by nature alone. It is by the exception to the course of nature that God *speaks*. Hence all irrational nature holds within itself that power to speak in the name of God. This being the case, it is not only possible, but *antecedently probable* that miracles should be wrought; for if they were never wrought, that power of nature would forever lie idle and unused.

Topics for Discussion. Hypnotism. Spiritism. The de Rudder cure. Hume's case against miracles. The compatibility of the necessity of physical laws with the exercise of freedom. When one man persuades another to act does he do so by the application of physical energy, or in accordance with the "necessary" course of nature? When does divine suasion of the human will attain the order of the miraculous? Ordinary Providence in human affairs not miraculous. Deists and Theists.

REFERENCES

Cath. Ency. "Miracle."
Cath. Record, Vol. 8, p. 340. "Explanation of Miracles by Unknown Forces of Nature."
Cath. World, Vol. 15, p. 133. "Newman on Miracles."

Commonweal, Vol. 2, p. 77. "Huxley and the Catholic Church."

Gerard, J. *Old Riddle and the Newest Answer.*

Irish Theol. Quarterly, Vol. 31, p. 1. "Miracles."

Joyce, G. *The Question of Miracles.*

Marsh, G. *Miracles.*

Month. Vol. 35, p. 491, "Hume and Huxley." Vol. 124, p. 561, and Vol. 125, p. 113, "Contemporary Miracles."

Newman, Card. *Two Essays on Miracles.*

Schanz, P. *A Christian Apology*, Vol. 2.

Windle, B. *On Miracles and Other Matters.*

CHAPTER XVI

MIRACLES RECOGNIZABLE

MIRACLES TO BE KNOWN. Since the purpose of miracles as such is to serve as a sign, it stands to reason that they must be capable of recognition, otherwise they should have no justification for their existence. For if a sign cannot be known it cannot be a sign. The degree of certitude we may have, need not, however, always be absolute. Moral certitude, or even a high degree of probability, suffices to justify a miracle. Still, when God chooses to make demands which may require great sacrifices, as when He commands adherence to His Church, we have a right to expect that the miracles will leave no reasonable doubt that God has so commanded. In the present thesis we merely seek to show that in some cases at least miracles can be recognized as such with certainty. When we say "as such," we mean that not only are we sure that the event occurred but that it occurred by special intervention of God.

THE THREE VERITIES. The verity of a miracle includes, ordinarily, three truths; the historical, the philosophical, and the theological. The *historical truth* means that the event occurred, that it is an historical fact. The *philosophical truth* means that the event exceeds the power of visible creation. The *theological truth* means that the event is such as could not be attributed to an evil spirit. In the case of immediate witnesses to the event the historical truth has no place, for they have the evidences of their senses; mediate witnesses must rely on historical truth. It is not, of course, supposed that these truths can be known without *diligent inquiry*.

OPPONENTS. Aside from the adversaries mentioned in the preceding thesis, there are some who have especially concentrated their attacks on the knowability of miracles; for example, Hume, Rousseau, Laplace, Voltaire, Strauss, Renan. They repudiate the thought that historical testimony could ever be reliable when it reports a miraculous event; and when they admit any wonderful happening they maintain that future discoveries of science will show it to have been entirely natural.

Thesis 16. Miracles can be recognized as such

Argument. Miracles can be recognized as such if their historical, philosophical, and theological truth can be established. But these three verities can be established. Therefore . . .

The major. By the nature of the case and by common consent of the disputants these three points are the only ones to be settled.

The minor. (1) A miracle is, by definition, an event perceptible by the senses. It therefore offers the best evidence available for any event, for we cannot require any greater evidence for an external fact than that we *saw, heard,* and *handled* the proofs. In fact, there will be greater attention paid to an unusual event than to an ordinary one, and it will attract a greater number of witnesses. Others who are not immediate witnesses can make sure of the occurrence in the same way they establish any other historical fact.

(2) To ascertain the philosophical truth we must make certain that the event could not be the result of natural forces either left to themselves or employed by the skill of man. To make sure of this is by no means impossible, for although we do not know everything that these forces can do, we know what, under certain circumstances, they *cannot do;* and we know many things which they cannot do under *any circumstances.* We know, for instance, that the sound of the human voice cannot cure leprosy, or restore life to a corpse corrupting in the grave.

(3) In order to establish the theological truth of a miracle we have only to exclude the agency of any *malign spirit* or spirits, who may perpetrate a marvel without the command, coöperation or approval of God. Since these spirits are creatures under the dominion of God, He *cannot allow* them perfectly to simulate His own deeds; otherwise they could frustrate the whole purpose of His creation. Therefore if evil spirits effect any prodigy there will always be about it something to enable us to distinguish it from an act of God. For example, the conditions of observation will be dubious or suspicious, the effect will be transient, the means or circumstances will be frivolous and unbecoming, the persons who sponsor the display will be of at least uncertain moral character, the ultimate effects will be to foster pride and vice, and far from being benef-

icent the whole ensemble and purpose of the event will be opposed to the honor of God and the good of man.

Difficulties. 1. The happenings at modern spiritistic seances are ascribed to other-world agencies; yet they have often on investigation been discovered to be due to fraud. The same may be true of so called miracles.

Reply. No one ever regarded spiritistic happenings as miracles in our sense, for not even the promoters claim that they are acts of God. Where we differ from the Spiritists is this: we are convinced that ordinarily the perpetrators of these phenomena are none other than the entirely human tricksters who are conducting the seance, while the believing Spiritists accept the effects as due to some agency in the invisible world. Still, were the Spiritists right in their belief, they would substantiate the possibility of extramundane intervention, without undermining the recognizability of true miracles. Phenomena which no one adduces as interventions on the part of God do not even invite examination on the score of their being miracles.

2. Before we can recognize a miracle as such we must first know all the forces of nature; but we can never know them, or at least never know that we do know them all. Therefore we can never know miracles as such.

Reply. We must know all the effects nature can produce under all circumstances, I deny. We must know what effects it *cannot* produce under given circumstances, I grant; and this last is sufficient to recognize a miracle as such.

3. We do not even know what nature cannot do under a given set of circumstances.

Reply. Then we know *nothing* about physical laws; for if we neither know what nature can do nor what it cannot do under the circumstances, we know no law for it whatsoever.

4. Hume [1] argues thus: I have physical certitude that the miracle did not happen, and only moral certitude, the witness' testimony, that it did happen. But physical certitude prevails over moral certitude. Therefore I am certain that the miracle did not happen.

Reply. The first part of the major, that I have physical certitude, etc., is utterly false. Physical certitude assures us that certain things cannot be done by material forces alone, i.e., left to themselves, and acting necessarily. It does not deny that these things can be done by *other* forces. The second part of the major, I have only moral certitude, etc., is also false in most cases, for if I witness the event myself, or if I have the right kind of testimony, my certitude may be reduced to metaphysical certitude. Hume distracts his readers from these glaring falsehoods by a facile style.

5. Years ago people would have considered the radio a miracle. So also the things which we are inclined to regard as miraculous now, may turn out to be only natural.

Reply. If broadcasting could have been done years ago *without any such instruments* as we now use, it would have been considered miraculous, I grant. And it would be considered so to-day. If done with some such instruments, it would have been considered a miracle, I deny. It must be admitted that we cannot forecast what human ingenuity may be able to do with the forces of nature in the coming centuries. But that has no bearing on the recognizing of miracles. We have not to decide what human skill can do, or will be able to do, or has done in the past: we have only to settle the question that human skill *did not* do this. That is decided by an examination of the particular case.

6. Science has discovered that many cures are effected by suggestion, that is by entirely natural means.

Reply. The power of suggestion has been known from time immemorial. Modern science does not claim to have done more than perfect the methods, nor does it claim to

[1] *An Inquiry Concerning Human Understanding,* X.

have sounded the first warning against hasty judgments about the miraculous nature of certain cures. Benedict XIV, though he is by no means the first, has phrased the warning thus: "Some are cured of their diseases by a strong faith and a powerful imagination. . . . All that is freely granted, without casting any doubt on the cures that have been demonstrated to be truly miraculous." [2] There are certain cures which even the best methods of suggestion cannot effect; as, e.g., the instantaneous healing of broken bones. And no one surely will maintain that a corpse is susceptible to suggestion about returning to life.[3]

7. Many religions holding contradictory tenets claim a confirmation of their doctrines by miracle, e.g., Buddhists, Pagans, Gnostics, Albigensians. But these cannot all be true miracles.

Reply. It is not for us here to decide which are true miracles, and which not; but only to lay down the conditions under which they can be recognized. The fact that so many appeal to miracles confirms the deep conviction men have that miracles are possible and knowable.

8. There has always been a brilliant school of writers who discountenance miracles.

Reply. More brilliant than profound, or even honest. Witness the case of Emile Zola, who pretending to write an historical novel about a cure at Lourdes, has the heroine cured, but afterwards allows her to die of the disease she thought herself cured of. That is, in the story she dies; although in real life, the original was still living at the time

---

[2] *De beat. et canon*, IV, p. 1, ad fin.

[3] Even though we cannot accept cures wrought by emotion as miraculous, we must not for that reason despise them all. Many of the cures at Lourdes fail of acceptance by the Medical Board as miraculous, in fact the very large majority of them fail so to be accepted. But such "rejected" cures are often a high tribute to the devotion of the pilgrim, as they are an honor to the Mother of God, or to the Blessed Sacrament, for evoking such supreme confidence.

the book was published, and had not a trace of the disease of which she had been cured.

Topics for Discussion. The assumption that future discoveries will reveal that "miracles" are due to entirely natural forces.   Cure by suggestion. Zola's treatment of the case of Marie Lebranchu.

REFERENCES

Catholic Record, Vol. 8, p. 340.   "Miraculous Manifestations."

Clifford, J. *The Logic of Lourdes* (America Press).

Irish Theol. Quart., Vol. 12, p. 34. "Evidence of the Supernatural."

Izard, F. *Medical Proof of the Miraculous.*

Grandmaison, L. de. *Twenty Cures at Lourdes.*

Jorgenson, J. *Lourdes.*

Newman, Card. *Apologia* (2nd ed.), p. 298.

PART III

THE SPECIFIC PROPERTIES OF BODIES

CHAPTER XVII

SCIENTIFIC ATOMISM. Philosophical Atomism must be distinguished from *Scientific Atomism*. We accept the latter; which teaches that all bodies (at least all inorganic bodies) are made up of infrasensible integral parts called molecules, atoms, electrons and protons and that even the ether itself is atomic, in the sense that from within the chemical atom it will radiate energy in a certain fixed quantum only, or some integral multiple of that quantum. This "atom of energy" is called Planck's quantum; it is represented by the symbol h, and is very minute; for, $h = 6.56 \times 10^{-27}$ ergs. The chemical atom is the unit of chemical activity.

PHILOSOPHICAL ATOMISM. What is most obvious in the teaching of scientific atomism is that bodies are made up of integral components in diminishing sizes. Such a condition was suspected long before it was discovered to be a fact. Democritus and his associate Leucippus in the fifth century B.C. proposed the theory that all bodies which come under observation are composed of invisible particles called atoms. These atoms were the *ultimate* particles; they could not be further divided. In so far forth Democritus has been borne out by modern

183

science. Now, it is important to notice that the
discovery of atoms has to do with one characteristic
only of bodies, their *quantity*. For atoms are integral parts, and *as such* do not imply activity, but
only the irreducible quantitative unit. Concentration on this phase of material substance is what has
misled Philosophical Atomists from Democritus to
the present day. Hence *Philosophical Atomism
teaches that material substance is nothing more than
concrete quantity without any intrinsic forces.*[1] It
follows from the above tenet, that, since one quantity, or extension, can differ from another only in
size and shape, all quantities being otherwise homogeneous, the sole manner in which one atom may
differ from another is in respective size and shape.
Again, since there are ultimate atoms, these atoms
must be undivided; otherwise they should be neither
ultimate nor atoms. For, although division implies
quantity, the fact of division does not destroy quantity; it destroys the atom, as atom, and makes it
cease to be ultimate. Hence, the Atomists, wishing
to hold to the theory of ultimate atoms, made these
atoms not only undivided but indivisible. That is
precisely what they meant by the name "atom."
They did not mean by this that the atoms are inextended, as the Dynamists maintain. The Atomists
held that the atoms, though very small, are truly
extended. Nor did they mean that you could not
project a division of an atom, as a bricklayer might
mark a brick where he intended to divide it; there
is ground for such designation even in the smallest

---

[1] We say concrete quantity in order to distinguish it from the
abstract extension dealt with in geometry.

atom, but the Atomists denied that you could ever effect the division by actually severing the parts. In other words atoms *resisted* division. Here is exactly where the Atomist surreptitiously departed from his original principle that material substance is merely concrete quantity. Resistance to division does not belong to quantity; it is a *force*. Quantity as such does not suffer by division, division does not destroy it, there is as much of it after the division as before. Quantity may be said, indeed, to resist compression, for compression directly attacks quantity, and if carried out would annihilate the quantity. And, of course, the Atomists held that atoms are incompressible.[2]

DIFFERENCE AND CHANGE. In keeping with their concentration on quantity, the Atomists reduced all the *differences* in observable bodies to the size, shape and relative position of the component atoms, and all *change* to purely local motion, and in accord with their principle of avoiding "force" narrowed the conditions of change down to simple impact. On the other hand, the *stability* of bodies was due to the interlocking of atoms. Atoms by reason of their irregular outlines, or hooklike surfaces, got caught in one another, and so formed an assemblage or constellation of greater or less magnitude according to the size of the resulting physical body. Hence again we notice that the Atomists adroitly introduced cohesive force, for no atom could grip another unless both had internal cohesion. From this analysis

[2] As is evident, we are here taking quantity as synonymous with three-dimensional extension, not the radical quantity considered in Thesis 9.

of the Atomists' doctrine we see. that they regarded all atoms as homogeneous with one another in the fact of extension, as differing only in those modifications which have direct reference to extension, and all of them without internal directive force, but depending entirely on how they get knocked about or get lodged in a swarm of other atoms. As Aristotle judged them[3] the Atomists did not recognize true efficient, final or formal cause, and had only an imperfect notion of material cause.

HISTORY OF ATOMISM. The history of Atomism shows that it has been held in varying degrees from the earliest times down to our own day. *Democritus* and *Leucippus,* following the Later Ionic School, rejected the thesis of the Earlier Ionian School that all matter is alive, and the thesis of the Eleatics that change is an illusion, and asserted that there is nothing but "brute" matter and no change but local motion. They supposed the universe to consist of the "full" and the "void," both real beings. The atoms constituted the "full," and their motion was due to their falling through the void, the heavier atoms falling faster than the lighter. Atoms by impinging upon one another gave rise to variety of motion. Even the soul of man was composed of merely the finer atoms. After Aristotle had criticized the system,[4] *Epicurus* returned to it, but modified the statement about different velocities in the "void." *Lucretius* brought Atomism to Rome. In the Middle Ages certain *Arab professors,* teaching at Bagdad and at Cordova, held Atomism, but attributed the motion directly to God. Each of these schools was opposed respectively by Avicenna and Averroes. Among Christian philosophers the following men have professed Atomism in a greater or less degree: *Francis Bacon,*

[3] *Metaph.* XII (XI). 2.
[4] *Phys.* IV. 8.

Descartes and the *Occasionalists, Gassendi, Hobbes, Locke,
Secchi* (for inorganic matter only),, *Büchner, Hæckel.*
Atomism has always been the favorite theory of the
Materialistic philosophers, for the reason that it puts the
question of purposive finality farther into the background.
In the present-day revolt against Materialism, many writers,
following Bergson, are reverting to the Early Ionian theory
that all matter is organic. Thus Whitehead holds that the
world is made up of organisms within organisms, even down
to the electron.[5]

SCIENTIFIC VIEWS. We have purposely omitted the
scientists from the history of Atomism, because they are not
directly concerned with the philosophical question. The
particular natural sciences are at pains only to discover the
integral parts of bodies and to formulate the *laws* according
to which the parts and the whole body act. But philosophy
must search as far as human understanding may take it into
the primary sources, or principles, of all the phenomena of
nature; thus the result of philosophical inquiry is to reach
the foundations which underlie all the particular sciences,
and philosophy cannot be satisfied that it has discovered these
foundations until its findings are in accord not only with one
or other science or group of sciences, but with the reliable
data of all the sciences. The scientific view is narrower.
If, for instance, a special branch of science or applied
mathematics finds it serviceable for its particular purpose to
consider matter only quantitatively, it need have no scruple
in doing so; omission of other factors is not a denial. Still,
scientists sometimes become so accustomed to their specialized
view and the terminology that goes with it that they speak
as though they were giving a complete report of the whole
reality of material substance. Hence we should be wary of
classifying among the Atomists such men as Newton, Maxwell, J. J. Thomson. It happens not infrequently that

[5] Cf. *Science and the Modern World*, p. 115.

scientists, when they philosophize, even mistake their own position. An example of this is Millikan, who says,[6] "To-day there is absolutely no philosophy in the field other than atomic philosophy, at least among physicists." That statement is based on a mistaken notion. Non-atomic philosophy does not deny that larger natural bodies may be made up of smaller and heterogeneous components. Aristotle, the founder of distinctly non-atomic philosophy, did not object to atoms; he objected to the kind of *union* the atoms formed in the theory of Democritus; Aristotle claimed that a mere flocking together could never result in anything but a mixture, could never form a compound which you could define as one natural body.[7] As long as we continue to recognize the difference between a mixture and a compound, we must concede that Aristotle was correct. Another misinterpretation of Aristotle is occasioned by his saying that when we divide a quantity into parts the parts retain the same nature which the undivided total had. But we now know that when we divide a molecule into atoms, the atoms do not have the same nature as the molecule. Aristotle, however, only meant, as we have seen,[8] that the parts have quantity as truly as the original had quantity. He did not mean that if, e.g., you divided a horse in two you should have two horses. To base the opposition between Aristotle and Lucretius on such misunderstanding of Aristotle, as Sir Wm. Bragg does,[9] is totally misleading. Thus we cannot always accept a writer's own account of where he stands on the question of Philosophical Atomism.

KINDS OF PHILOSOPHICAL ATOMISM. *Materialistic* atomism holds that matter has no true efficient forces, but is possessed only of motion which is im-

[6] *The Electron*, p. 15.
[7] Cf. *Metaph.* VIII (VII). 2.
[8] Thesis 6.
[9] *Concerning the Nature of Things,* Ch. I.

parted by transfer and seeks an equilibrium.[10] To
this is usually added nowadays blind "evolution,"
in order to exclude the possibility of an extramundane directive Cause. *Mechanical* Atomism con-
cedes to matter the efficient powers of attraction
and repulsion, but does not differentiate these powers in any other way.[11] In this school Descartes and
the Occasionalists appealed to the Creator as the
direct cause of the activities of matter. *Moderate*
Atomism grants atoms many forces, but holds that
they retain their individuality.[12]

MATTER IN MODERN SCIENCE. Matter as revealed by modern discoveries is decidedly atomic,
but in a sense entirely different from that of the
Atomism of old. Instead of ascribing bare extension and only passive properties to matter, many
modern scientists are inclined to make matter synonymous with energy and activity. Still, as we have
noted in Thesis 8, these theories do not represent
the classical Dynamism any more than they represent Atomism. In order to see how atomic matter
is considered to be, it is necessary for us only to
recall how crystals are composed of molecules,
molecules composed of atoms, atoms of protons
and electrons. These last named go in pairs; a
single pair make up the hydrogen atom, and the
numbers range upward through the periodic table
until two hundred and thirty-eight protons and the
same number of electrons are required to constitute
the atom of uranium. This is not all. The very

[10] Cf. Thesis 12.
[11] Thus, Empedocles, Tongiorgi, and many philosophical
physicists.
[12] Thus Avicenna.

ether which fills the relatively vast spaces between
the particles of ponderable matter would itself seem
to be in a certain sense atomic. For the electrons,
according to the Bohr theory, will not travel except
in certain fixed orbits; they cannot be made to vary
infinitesimally from their course, they *jump*. Each
orbit represents a certain quantity of energy, and
the electrons by jumping from one orbit to another
enable the atom to absorb or release a fixed amount
of energy. It has been discovered that there is a
minimum quantum, an *atom of energy* so to speak;
the atom may radiate or absorb various multiples of
this minimum quantum, but never a fraction. As a
result of all this the doctrine which is gaining favor
to-day is the electrical theory of matter, which suggests that all matter is electricity. Thus Berthoud
says, "Matter is nothing more than energy in an
extremely condensed form and endowed with a special structure." [13]   On this theory ponderable matter, which consists of minute particles at relatively
great distances apart, is simply so many centers of
intense concentrations of electricity. Some vary the
statement by calling the particles concentrations of
ether. It is further supposed that these centers or
"knots" may, by means as yet only guessed at, be
unraveled into any of the commoner forms of energy.
It is expected, too, that this unraveling must come
in jumps, or atoms. We need not delay over the
data for these theories nor weigh their reliability.
It is evident that the only thing left from the old
Atomism is that matter is atomic. But philosophers
never quarreled over that. They quarreled over the

[13] *New Theories of Matter and the Atom*, p. 101.

question whether matter is active or whether it is *only passive*. To modern science matter is so far from being a "dead" thing, capable only of being thrust about, that it is regarded as essentially *energizing* and *highly cohesive*.

Our present thesis is directed against Philosophical Atomism; and, in that field, if we prove our case against the Materialistic, or Extreme, Atomists, we shall have accomplished enough to establish our next thesis. Extreme Atomism seeks to reduce all the phenomena of matter to concrete quantity, rejecting all active forces; if it sticks to its last, it must account for all the properties of bodies by (a) *incompenetration,* an attribute of quantity, (b) variations of *extension,* such as size, shape, position, collocation, etc., and (c) *motion* of varying speed and direction. In our proof we shall endeavor also to show the weakness of Mechanical Atomism. And although we might use arguments from vegetative and sense life with much more telling effect than arguments from the inorganic world, still we shall confine ourselves to the latter as abundantly sufficient to overthrow the contention of the Atomists. The reasoning is then *a fortiori* for the organic world.

Thesis 17. Philosophical Atomism cannot account for the characteristic properties of the distinct types of material substance

Argument 1. Distinct and set types of material substances are evidenced by (a) the physical laws, (b) finality, (c) cohesion, (d) efficient activity, (e) affinity, (f) chemical combination, and (g) chemical decomposition. But Philosophical Atomism fails to explain any of these characteristics. Therefore Philosophical Atomism cannot account for the characteristic properties of the distinct types of material substance.

The major. (a) Physical laws are tendencies in matter; but some matter has one tendency, other matter another tendency; and in each case the tendency is fixed and determined. This variety of fixed tendencies sets matter off from matter as distinct in type. (b) Finality is exhibited in the way material substance maintains its integrity, or failing that fits in aptly with a higher and more complicated order. But such precision in the aptitudes of matter to achieve countless examples of complex order (e.g., atom, molecule, crystal) is inexplicable without fixity of types in at least the original matter. (c) The fact that we can speak of a body at all in the singular number, even of the ultimate atom, means that certain portions of matter hold together sufficiently to be recognized as in some way distinct from the rest of matter. Without that distinction there could, of course, be no types of matter, but with it we see that these individual portions fall into certain set types, as gold, iron, lead, etc. (d) Granted the fact of efficient activity, as proved in Thesis 12, and granted its necessity and constancy as displayed in the course of nature, we have here only to note that efficiency is limited to a fixed measure and mode; a proton has only a certain "pull," and that is exercised with a definite measure of strength and on an electron; another proton it will repel. The same is true of efficiency throughout nature; it is specified as to the measure and the object on which it is exercised. This specified activity is an index of the nature of matter under observation, and compels us to classify matter into distinct types. (e) Chemical affinity, e.g., the marked tendency of Cl to unite with H, whether it be immediately due to the structure of the atoms or not, is a very selective and discriminating activity by which chemists universally recognize distinct types of substance. It is an intrinsic and invariable activity which endures regardless of contingent conditions. (f) Chemical compounds are formed by certain fixed ratios of certain fixed ingredients. This itself is sufficient to indicate that the ingredients belong to set types. But the compounds themselves fall exactly into distinct groups and classes. (g) The fact that the resultants of chemical decomposition are identical in ratio and kind with the materials before composition is a clinching corroboration of the fixity of types of matter.

The minor. A. *Extreme Atomism.* Motion imparted by impact is *indefinitely variable,* depending upon the point at which the impact occurred. The motion on which Extreme Atomism bases its contention has its counterpart in the motion of molecules in a gas. It is perfectly clear that no fixity of types can result from such *indiscriminate* movement. Hence all that definiteness which we have described in explaining the major of our argument is left totally unaccounted for by Extreme Atomism. In particular the cohesion of the ultimate particles which sustain the impact is left unexplained. Without *cohesion* the impact of two bodies would dissipate them into infinitesimal dust. Quantity is not destroyed, but it must be completely shattered if there be no force to hold it together. Still, Atomism discards force of this sort. The motive force accepted by Atomism, moreover, but called "transfer," cannot explain the *selective* activity of chemicals, for motion does not select its object; nor can it explain why combinations are never formed except in definite ratios, for moving bodies may flock together in any ratio; it cannot explain how the resultants of decomposition exactly correspond to the original ingredients, for the original motions lose their identity entirely in the combined motion, and although that combined motion may be resolved into constituents, the *original* constituents are only one set against an infinite number; any one of the originals has only that vanishing chance to reappear, and the whole set has less of a chance to come back together. On this theory, then, there can be no laws, no order, no knowledge of, nor any sense to nature.

B. *Mechanical Atomism.* This kind of Atomism wishes to reduce the activities of matter to *attraction* and *repulsion,* something akin to the "love" and "hate" of Empedocles. Now, though attraction and repulsion are basic characteristics of matter, the properties we know cannot be accounted for in such bare terms. Mere attraction is exemplified in gravitation, and repulsion in electric charges of the same sign. Matter as we know it, even inorganic matter, is not a mere congeries of "solar systems." The attraction and repulsion of nature is very *highly qualified*. We have seen that in the study of the

atom, of the compound molecule and the crystal.
The ultimate particles of matter as well as the
larger units act in too distinctly specified a manner to be governed by the simple forces of attraction and repulsion. Solar systems are not made up
like atoms, nor is it conceivable that a union of them
could form anything comparable to a molecule or
crystal in structure and natural completeness. Hence,
on the bare postulate of attraction and repulsion, we
could never build up a system of *laws* such as hold
for all the known activities of matter; nor could
such a postulate account for the evident *finality* of
action, for finality preserves the natural units by
intrinsic tendency, or if forced by extrinsic conditions to sacrifice that unity does so only in favor of
another natural unit with an intrinsic tendency of
its own. Mere attraction and repulsion are too
vague and general to achieve these distinctive
results.[14] For the rest, it is sufficient to mention the
different *kinds of cohesion,* the *limit of valency,* the
discrimination of *affinity,* and the *ratio of composition;* these characteristics cannot be explained by the
two sweeping principles of attraction and repulsion;
these two forces exist, but they are not always at
play, and when they do act they are under a very
definite control from within the agent itself. Hence,
Mechanical Atomism, though it admits active forces,
still fails to account for the distinct types of natural
bodies.

Argument 2. Materialistic Atomism is practi-
cally based on the principle that we should not accept

---

[14] We indeed hold finality in the relation of the earth to the
sun, but only because of the original collocation of matter in the
universe, not because of an intrinsic tendency in matter.

forces because we cannot see them. But that is not a valid basis for the theory. Therefore it is to be rejected.

The minor. We can see the effect of forces, and that is amply sufficient reason for accepting them. Moreover, Atomism must accordingly reject the ether, which we are told occupies more than a million times the volume occupied by ponderable matter even within the compass of the atom. Likewise it must reject atoms themselves, for they are invisible by any means we know.

Topics for Discussion. Comparison of Ionian and Atomist theories. Did Democritus postulate what could properly be called elements? How did he account for diversity and change? Stahl's "phlogiston."

REFERENCES

Cath. Ency. "Atomism."

Ency. Brit. "Chemistry."

Nys, D. In *Manual of Modern Scholastic Philosophy.* "Cosmology," Part 1, Ch. 1.

O'Neill, J. *Cosmology,* Vol. 1, Chs. 1, 2.

Turner, W. *History of Philosophy.* Section B, Chs. 1, 4, 5.

CHAPTER XVIII

SUBSTANTIAL FORM

THE POINT UNDER DISCUSSION. The age-old discussion of substantial form has always involved two questions: (1) is there substantial form? and (2) if so, is that form distinct from mere matter? Much confusion arises from discussing the two questions simultaneously. We shall therefore in this thesis consider only the first question, leaving the second for treatment in the next number. And since the second question has, historically, revolved about the nature of change, we may also put that subject aside for the present. Meanwhile we shall accept change as a fact without discussing its implications in regard to question 2. It is our single purpose here to establish substantial form *as an alternative to Materialistic Atomism,* and not as opposed to mere matter.

ATOMS NOT UNDER DISPUTE. It cannot be too forcibly emphasized that the difference between Philosophical Atomism and the doctrine of substantial form does not consist in the acceptance of atoms by one and their rejection by the other. There exists a widespread persuasion to that effect, but it is only another example of how a mere name like "Atomism" will for some writers serve to justify a whole system of philosophy. Aristotle who first formulated the doctrine of substantial form, did not object to Democritus' atoms; he objected to accepting the *kind of union* those atoms formed in the theory of Democritus. As we have seen, if nature worked on the lines laid down by Atomism the result would always be an indiscriminate mixture, and no perceptible body could ever stand out as belonging, with multitudes of others, to a distinct type. Aristotle knew, as we all do, that such a system cannot be accepted as a rational account of the phenomena of nature. With what we now know about the structure of matter down to the minutest particles, there is no scientist to-day who is willing to swallow Atomism whole.

FORM. Substantial form is a name which has perhaps proved no less misleading, to non-Aristotelian philosophers at least, than has the term "Atomism." Form, in the common acceptation of the word, is the figure or contour of an object. This kind of form is a means by which to discriminate objects, and classify them. Thus the letters of the alphabet have each a form; all A's are alike regardless of their size, color or material; and all B's are alike, though distinctly different from the A's. Such forms, however, are accidents; not that they happen by accident, but they *are* accidents; they belong to that class of being. But we also classify objects according to another principle; two men are the same kind of being even if one be standing and the other seated. By what right do we call them the same? What is it which makes substances belong to one kind, and differ from another kind? Not the accidental form; that is a mere modification of the

quantity or extension; a quantity of wax may be in
the form of a sphere or in the form of a cube, but
in both conditions it is wax; a quantity of lead may
be cubical, too, but it is not wax. We can classify
objects according to their shape, but that is not
classifying substances. There is something which
makes certain substances alike, but distinctly different from all others. What causes that sameness
and that difference? It is something deeper and
more lasting than accidental form; and for want of
a better word Aristotle called it *"substantial"* form.

SUBSTANTIAL FORM. *Substantial form,* then, is
that radical character or determinant which puts
matter in a definite natural species. The form is
often called by Aristotle the "species." [1] We have
frequently remarked that mere quantity, incompene-
trability and local motion are universal attributes
of matter. We cannot distinguish matter from matter, as to *kind,* by these properties. To know to
what species a body belongs we must detect some
properties that are characteristic of that species
only, we must ascertain some specific properties.
Thus gold is yellow, very ductile, has a certain specific gravity, melts at a certain temperature, is not
affected by sulphuric acid, etc. That which gives
rise to these specific properties, the primary origin
or principle of them, is substantial form. Form,
therefore, is that which gives matter a certain determined kind of existence. But are these sets of properties themselves identical with substantial form?
The obvious answer is No; because they are accidents. These properties are, it is true, a different

[1] Cf. *De An.* II. 1.

kind of accidents than mere shape. They are inseparable properties, not simply variable conditions of
the subject. Still they are accidents, for they are
modes of the subject; and if they were substances
they should have to be many substances in one. But,
though they are accidents, they do for that reason
imply something deeper, further back, from which
they spring. That *root-cause of the specific properties* is substantial form.

SCIENCE AND SUBSTANCE. The idea of substance
expounded in the last paragraph is not an innova-
tion, nor is it a notion foreign to science. A. Smith
defines substance as "a species of matter, with a
constant set of properties." [2] The fact that a particular set of properties is constant indicates a species, and that species is called a substance. Furthermore since sets of properties differ, it follows that
there are specifically different substances; different
species are different substances. The root-cause
which makes them different substances is substantial
form.

SPECIFIC DIFFERENCE. It is of importance next
to note what we mean by difference. Two nuggets
of gold, we say, are exactly alike in substance, they
are the same species of matter; but they are different from lead, for the lead belongs to another species. We do not, however, mean that the two nuggets of gold are exactly identical; one is here and
the other is a yard away; they are not the same
piece of gold. Thus we may have two specimens of
the same species, which *differ within the species*. The
difference is not specific. We need not go any fur-

[2] *College Chemistry*, p. 7.

ther than that in the present discussion, for we are
satisfied to recognize a *difference between species.*
Nevertheless, in order to make clear what we
mean by specific difference, it will be helpful to
study the other kind of substantial difference. When
I say that I have two individual specimens of the
same species, I signify that each specimen is a substance; they are substantially the same in species and
substantially different as individuals. I recognize
the different individuals by the fact that they occupy
separate portions of space. But is the nugget of
gold an individual? I may cut the lump in two with
my knife, and each section is gold as before.
I could continue dividing, by whatever means might
be possible, until I had reached the ultimate molecules, without changing the species.

NATURE AND SUBSTANCE. The word "nature"
is often used in a broad sense to designate any characteristics of an object, but in the strict sense it
means a substance. In this strict sense the thing
pointed out by the term is not an accident but a substance. If I say "nature" and then say "substance,"
the material objects of the two concepts is the same
concrete thing; only the formal objects differ; nature
and substance are two aspects of the same material
object; "substance" is silent about activity, "nature"
asserts activity. A substance, then, considered in
respect to its normal activities is a nature; a nature
considered as independent of a subject in which to
inhere is a substance. There cannot be a plurality
of natures in one substance, nor a plurality of substances in one nature; because both, though from
different points of view, designate the same one

being. No substance exists without being capable of
action, for such a substance could have no purpose
and could not make itself known to us; hence every
substance is, as a matter of fact, a nature. Now,
the normal and characteristic activities of a substance represent its distinctive nature, and these
activities we call specific properties. Specific properties are (1) a particular *kind* of activity, i.e., they
each have a certain class of object on which they are
exercised; and (2) they have a more or less well-
defined *limit*, i.e., they cannot exercise their efficiency in an illimitable manner, they have a certain
amount of power, and no more. These properties
owe their specific character to the substantial form,
which may therefore be rightly called the *substantial
nature* of a given portion of matter.

Substantial Form a Cause. It was in Aristotle's quest for causes that he became convinced of
the insufficiency of the Atomist doctrine.[3] In the
atomistic scheme there was no cause for the *fixity of
specific properties*. Aristotle also reasoned that a
cause must ultimately be something substantial;
hence when he named the cause of the specific properties "form," he wished it to be understood as
belonging to the order of substance, and not accident.[4] It is not merely a principle of these properties, for principle signifies only priority in general.
Cause signifies that the prior has an intrinsic connection with the subsequent, which in that case is
called the effect. The intrinsic connection consists in
the fact that the effect, as we have noted before,

[3] Cf., e.g., *Metaph.* I. 1; VIII (VII). 4; VII (VI). 3.
[4] Cf. *Metaph.* VII (VI). 7, 17.

owes its existence to the cause. There need not be priority of time; but naturally the subsequent presupposes the antecedent. Actions are accidents and presuppose substance; specific accidents presuppose a specific substance. That which specifies the substance is its substantial form, or, in other words, its nature. Substantial form is the *cause* of the properties in so far as they are of a certain *kind* and have a certain *limit*. Thus substantial form is called the "primary actuality," to distinguish it from the subsequent actualities, which, because they are actions, are accidents.

OPPONENTS OF THE THESIS. The only adversaries of the thesis are the *Extreme Atomists,* and they are so indirectly, or by default, because they stop short of giving any reason for the specific properties of matter.

Thesis 18. The various types of inorganic matter as they occur in nature cannot be explained except by substantial form

Argument. Inorganic matter is not found except in certain well-defined types. But these types cannot be explained except by substantial form. Therefore inorganic matter cannot be explained except by substantial form.

The major. There is no portion of matter in the inorganic state which the chemist cannot classify as one of the elements or as a definite compound; and if there are some substances which have not as yet been classified, that is never considered as a reason why it cannot be done; science is certain that there is no molecule of matter which is not a type for, or a replica of, millions of other molecules of one distinct class. Inorganic matter does not shade off continuously from one kind into another; the lines of demarcation are clear-cut and abrupt. Science does not know matter except in classes.

These types are (a) natural species, (b) of a certain stability, and (c) definite final tendency.

(a) A natural species is had when there are numerous specimens which are exactly alike, except that they occupy different portions of space. This is the case with every inorganic substance we know; if it be divided down even to the ultimate crystals, or the ultimate molecules, the specimens are all alike; in the two instances given they are even of the same size and structure; the only way we can discriminate them is to say that one is here and another there.

(b) We do not claim that all the types have equal stability; but they all have at least *some* stability, and a very *definite amount* for all the specimens of each type. Thus the stability of each compound under given conditions is a thing which can be exactly reckoned. The same is true of the elements, and some of them are so stable, e.g., neon, that we have not been able as yet to make them enter into any chemical combination.

(c) This final tendency we have discussed in Theses 2 and 17. Amid all the changes of types in the inorganic world perfect order and aptitude is always preserved. The success of all the processes of nature, and especially of corporeal life, depends on this fixed fitness of the various types of inorganic matter.

The minor. But these facts cannot be explained

by mere extrinsic and indefinitely variable conditions; they cannot but be due to some principle *intrinsic to the matter* which has the above mentioned
characters. Because:

(a) Man has always most aptly described different
matter as having different natures; and by *nature* is
meant something *intrinsic* in the subject referred to.
The fact that so many specimens of the same species
occur in the world about us is positive proof that
the reason is something *within the matter itself,* and
not merely the result of how the matter happened
to be jostled about. External conditions, indeed,
affect matter, but it *reacts only in certain definite
ways,* which again is evidence of an *internal principle*
of activity. If changes occur in the species, the
resulting substance or substances can still be recognized as specimens of well-defined species; so that
reaction of this most radical type (i.e., chemical
change) is always dictated by the *inner nature* of the
matter involved, regardless of what external conditions occasioned the change. Deeply as modern
science has probed into the constitution of matter,
it has always found that it is the components themselves which *select* the constituents of the atom, molecule or crystal; that they *stop* short at a definite
number; that they arrange themselves in a certain
structure, presenting the particle as a complete unit;
and that this unit is a member of a species, where it
has countless other perfect replicas of itself. This
exact determination, even in the minutest particles
of matter, cannot be effected except by *intrinsic
forces* of a very definite kind and measure. The
deeper we penetrate into matter the more evi-

dence we have that its species is determind *from
within*.

(b) If all types of matter were merely the results
of chance collocations of atoms there could be no
reason why one type should be *more stable* than
another, or why one type should always have the
same stability. But we know that each type has a
fixed stability. The coal in the firebox of a locomotive will burn, at the temperature developed there,
but the iron firebox itself will not. There is some
very definite property within the matter itself which
determines under what external conditions, and at
what point (e.g., of temperature) it will undergo
chemical change. And although it seems to be true
that the stability of the various elements and compounds depends on the arrangement of the electrons
in the atom, and of the atoms in the molecule, that
very arrangement is, as we have seen, determined
ultimately by the innate, selective, limited forces of
the primitive components. Hence the stability is
due to an *intrinsic principle*.

(c) Finality is exhibited by the stability of the
type and by its specified reaction toward the production of other useful types. And unless we wished
to hold, with the Occasionalists, that God Himself
directly acts on the matter to keep the components
together or to put them into union with other components, we must grant that the forces which do this
are intrinsic to matter.

Our proof of the minor in the original syllogism
has thus far amounted to this: the types of inorganic matter cannot be explained except by an intrinsic principle. All that remains is to show that the

intrinsic principle is rightly called substantial. These forces which account for the types are either accidents or they are substance. If they be substance, then they themselves constitute the specific substantial nature of the matter in question. If they are accidents, then they must be proper accidents, genuine properties; for we cannot radically extinguish them in matter, and we never find matter without them. They therefore emanate from substance, and declare a substantial specific nature back of them. The ultimate principle is consequently substantial form.

Difficulties. 1. Aristotle did not know anything about atoms and molecules, electrons and protons. Hence, to seek to apply his system to the data of modern science is, on the face of it, absurd.

Reply. That Aristotle did not know *as much about* atoms as we do, I grant; that Aristotle did not have any notion of the existence of atoms, I deny. Almost a century before Aristotle's time Democritus had postulated atoms, and Aristotle did not quarrel with the postulate as such. He objected that the obvious natural unity and differences of material bodies could never be adequately explained by the haphazard flocking together of atoms. His complaint was that this did not give a full account of what is evident in nature, namely that an indiscriminate concourse of atoms cannot yield fixed classes and order, and that on the theory of Democritus nothing in the material world could be *defined.*[5]

2. Among the elements there are many *isotopes,* i.e., atoms with the same chemical properties, but different weights; and *isobars,* i.e., atoms of the same weight and different chemical properties. These latter have a counterpart in the *isomers,* which are compound molecules, made up of the same atoms in the same ratio, yet having altogether different

[5] Cf. *Metaph.* VIII (VII). 2.

properties. But these facts destroy the claim that there are species in the inorganic world.

Reply. In the language of science, the chemical properties depend on the net positive charge on the nucleus; hence, if one pair of components (electron and proton) are subtracted from the nucleus, the net charge there remains the same, the electrons in the periphery, or outer shell, are the same, and consequently the chemical properties remain unchanged; but the weight differs because of the parts subtracted, and the atom is an isotope. With an isobar the case is different; an electron passes from the nucleus to the periphery: that does not change the weight, but it changes the chemical properties. Thus uranium X_1 and uranium X_2 each contains 234 electrons (and 234 protons); but, in the case of the former, 144 of the electrons are in the nucleus, with 90 in the periphery; in the latter there is one less electron in the nucleus (which changes the nuclear charge), and one more in the periphery. The result is that the two isobars differ chemically, but not in weight. The different chemical behavior of isobars, as of isomers, is due proximately to the arrangement of the components. We admit all this freely on the authority of the scientists. But to say that this destroys species is untrue; these various types are just as clearly defined natural classes as are the more common types; and each has its own definite stability and specific properties. Hence, in answering the objection we deny the minor.

3. The atom, molecule and crystal, as we know them, are resultants of forces. But resultants of forces are never species.

Reply. That they are the mere resultant of forces, as that expression is used in mechanics, I deny. That their structure is a very specific result of specific forces, I grant. The "resultant of forces" is a bugaboo used to terrify those who would assert substantial form. If two projectiles flying at angles to one another were to meet in mid-air, and from that point move off as one projectile, the new path would represent a resultant of forces according to the familiar parallelogram. If we suppose the two projectiles to have so fused in the meeting as to be indistinguishable from one another, then the resultant could be analyzed into components of any number, size, direction, and velocities. In other words, this result could arise from any one of an infinite number of combinations. Nothing like this, however, happens in the production of atoms, molecules and crystals. Here is just the difference between Atomism and the doctrine of substantial form. Without going into the chemistry of it, the man in the street knows that the constantly uniform results of combinations must be due to *fixed interior forces;* and the chemist knows that they can be analyzed into only certain very *definite* components.

4. Man can arbitrarily form certain compounds, e.g., synthetic dyes, and these are artificial species. But with as much right may all species be called artificial, and purely a result of conditions.

Reply. Man proceeds in an arbitrary or "artificial" *manner,* and not as the necessarily acting forces of nature which, for instance, produces indigo. But for the result he depends on the innate forces of matter, and cannot achieve the result without them. If anything further were needed to disprove Atomism this fact alone would disprove it.

5. Substantial form is a cause; but a cause can produce very diverse effects; therefore substantial form can have a variety of effects. The consequence is that you cannot argue from different effects to different substantial forms.

Reply. An *efficient* cause, as such, can produce diverse effects. The formal cause limits the efficiency to a certain class of objects and a certain mode of acting. Natural agents do not merely act, they act in a *specified manner.* Within this specified manner countless agents act with perfect *uniformity.* This fixed uniformity calls for a reason intrinsic in the agents of each class. That intrinsic reason we call substantial form; it does not replace efficient cause; it pre-ordains the *kind* of effect the agent may produce. Hence where there are different kinds of effects, there must be different formal causes.

Topics for Discussion. Species in inorganic matter. Relation of formal to final cause. Form and nature; form and essence; form and substance. Specifically different forms as opposed to Monism.

REFERENCES

Cath. Ency. "Form."

Cath. World. Vol. 11, p. 54, "New Theory for Constitution of Matter." Vol. 19, pp. 577, 721, "Constitution of Matter."

Nys, D. In *Manual of Modern Scholastic Philosophy.*

Studies, Vol. 3, p. 301. "Most Recent Theories of Matter."

PART IV

THE ESSENTIAL COMPOSITION
OF BODIES

CHAPTER XIX

PARTS, INTEGRAL AND ESSENTIAL. The phenomena of the material world may be grouped under two headings, extension and activity. We have studied these two universal attributes of matter under their various phases, and are now to study how the two are combined in the same body. We call this combination *essential composition,* to distinguish it from *integral composition. Integral* parts are those which exist (or can exist) outside of one another in space. For example, the integral parts of man are the bodily members: hands, feet, head, etc. *Essential parts* are such that the removal of any one of them destroys the being; and they are of two kinds, metaphysical and physical. *Metaphysical parts* are those which are the results of mental precision; for example, animality and rationality in man. *Physical parts* are such as are distinct from one another independently of, and antecedently to, the mind's consideration, e.g., the soul and body. In the present thesis we grant that the two concepts "primary matter" and "substantial form" are distinct concepts, and that they are therefore metaphysical parts. What we seek to show is that they are also physical parts.

[1] This treatise may be omitted in an undergraduate course.

213

ORIGIN OF THE THEORY. The Atomists asserted only accidental change. The Eleatics denied that there is any change at all, and contended that change is an illusion. These latter argued that if there were change it must mean that new beings spring from nothing, very much as you might say, to use a modern illustration, that the moving pictures on the screen consist of a series of beings which spring from nothing and vanish into nothing. Aristotle refused to accept the views either of the Atomists or of the Eleatics. He maintained that changes are real, and that not merely new accidents come into existence but new substances as well. Still he could not argue that the new substances sprang from sheer nothingness into being, and then, when the next change ensued, lapsed back into nothingness. His answer was that material substance is made up of two parts, two essential physical components. One of these components, primary matter, does not change. The other component, substantial form, does change, or rather is exchanged. To put it briefly, matter exchanges one form for another.

TRANSMUTATION OF ELEMENTS. The reason for Aristotle's answer is found in the physics of his day. Physicists, following the lead of Empedocles, taught that there are four elementary substances: earth, air, fire and water. They further asserted that these elements were transmutable bodily into one another. They would say, for instance, that the earthy substance coal turned to fire, which turned to air, which turned, in the clouds, to water. That was crude physics, but it was all that Aristotle had, and he accepted it. Now, an element, if you take it

strictly, means a substance which is not a compound;
it cannot be dissolved into more primitive ingredients.   It cannot be changed into something else by
the disintegration of its parts or the rearrangement
of its components.   Hence in the transmutation of
elements the only thing that can happen is that one
elementary character ceases outright and is replaced
by the other.   Still Aristotle could not admit that
the entire being went out of existence, and another
entirely new being sprung up in its place.   Consequently he said that a part of the being, the matter,
remained; the other part, the form, ceased, and in
its place a new form sprang up in the matter.   Certainly, then, primary matter and substantial form
are distinct physically, because they are physically
separable.

WHAT ARE THE MODERN ELEMENTS?   On Aristotle's
premises his reasoning was logical enough.   But modern
physics has destroyed the premises.   First of all, the elements
are certainly not the four he accepted; secondly, it is difficult
for us to say which are the real elements; lastly, no matter
which substances we accept as elementary, there is no transmutation among them.[2]   What, then, are the modern elements?   If we answer that they are the ninety-odd chemical
elements named in our textbooks, we find that we have some
explanations to make.   The basis of that classification is the
ultimate minimum chemical agent; and that agent is the
atom of these substances.   Hence we must explain that
ordinary oxygen, for example, cannot be the real element,
because ordinary oxygen is diatomic.   The real chemical

[2] It must be remembered that these data of modern science do
not in any way lessen the evidence for substantial form, quite the
contrary.   But they destroy the old argument for the physical distinction between form and matter.

element is monatomic oxygen, quite a different substance. Again, the most modern physics would have us believe that the atoms of all the chemical elements are made up of the hydrogen atom, and that this latter is composed of one proton and one electron. Are, then, the protons and the electrons the ultimate elements? Even that has its difficulties. About the proton we know very little at all. As for the electrons, they behave in so peculiar a manner within the atom itself, that the ether, or the field in which they move, seems to have more to say about the atom than the very electrons. Witness the following from Kramers and Holst.[a] "During the transition from one stationary state to another we have no knowledge at all of the existence of the electron, indeed we do not even know whether it exists at the time or whether it perhaps is dissolved in the ether to be reformed in a new stationary state." Thus even the last object of our quest eludes our grasp. The only thing left is to retrace our steps to the atom of the chemical elements as being the best qualified for the rôle of real element, and provide all explanations by the name "chemical."

IS THERE TRANSMUTATION IN MODERN ELEMENTS? At first thought there seem to be many cases of transmutation in the chemical elements. *Radio-activity* is the disintegration of an atom by the emission of particles, with a change of character in the residue of the atom. Thus the end-result of radium is an isotope of lead. *Isomers* (molecules) and *isobars* (atoms) represent a change of character without any loss or addition of components, but merely by their rearrangement. *Isotopes* on the other hand do undergo a loss or addition of components, yet without change of chemical properties. These properties are determined by the net positive charge on the nucleus, and that remains the same in all the isotopes. The weight alone varies. Now,

[a] *The Atom and the Bohr Theory of its Structure*, p. 133.

if one of the isotopes of lead were to emit two alpha-particles [4] and one beta-particle, [5] the resulting product would be gold. Such transformation is being attempted. Another claimant for transmutation is *allotropy*. Allotropic forms are such as carbon in the forms of diamond, graphite and lampblack; or white and red phosphorus; or oxygen and ozone. The reasons of these differences are not well understood by chemists; but a most probable cause, which is verified in the case of oxygen and ozone, is that the number of atoms in the molecule determines the form. Oxygen is diatomic, ozone triatomic. In none of the above examples, however, is there any parallel to the transmutation supposed by ancient physics. Transmutation meant that one element converted other elements into itself, as fire was said to convert other things into fire. Of such transmutation of elements modern science does not afford us a single example. Neither may we think as some have [6] that the ancient elements were merely the common states of matters: solid (earth), liquid (water), gaseous (air), and incandescent (fire), and that transmutation was a change from one such state to another. That notion is sufficiently dispelled by Aristotle's statement [7] that ice is "frozen water." He still calls the element water, although it is in the solid state. In short, there is no transmutation known to us. The conversion of an electron into a proton would indeed be a case in point, but no scientist so much as hopes to achieve that. The upshot of all this is that the principal argument which Aristotle and the Scholastics relied upon to prove the physical distinction between matter and form is no longer available. [8]

[4] An alpha-particle is the same as the nucleus of the helium atom.
[5] An electron.
[6] E.g., Berthoud, *New Theories of Matter and the Atom*, p. 16.
[7] *Metaph*. III. 3.
[8] Cf. St. Th., *De gen. et cor*. I. 9.

PERSISTENCE OF THE ELEMENTS IN TRANSMU-
TATION. Although transmutation is now discredited,
it is instructive to study how such a change, if it
occurred, must take place, and what would be its
effect. Evidently the converting element must
act as the efficient cause in expelling the form of
the converted element, and in inducing its own form
in the matter thus taken over. The matter in this
case must be mere matter, "primary matter"; for
it is evident that an *elementary* form, because it is
elementary, cannot be resolved into other forms,
and must disappear entirely at the advent of another
elementary form. The properties of the converted
element are utterly abolished.

PERSISTENCE OF THE ELEMENTS IN THE COM-
POUND. Altogether different from transmutation
is the *formation of a compound*. In the former
case one element retained its substantial form
throughout the process. Now, as long as a material substance retains its substantial form it has
active properties and can act as an efficient cause.
It cannot act as efficient cause if it be reduced to
prime matter. If, then, we suppose two elements
are about to combine to form a compound, the substance which they are to form is not identical with
either element, but different from both. In this
case we cannot suppose that both elements are
stripped down to prime matter previous to the
advent of the form of the compound; for then
there could be no efficient cause to produce the new
form. There must be simultaneity of cause and
effect. But this cannot be if the causes go out of

existence, as causes, before the effect occur. Hence
the active properties of the elements must in some
way be simultaneous with the new form in the compound. Aristotle and his followers did not hold
that the properties of the elements disappeared
totally in the compound. Instead, they maintained
that the elementary properties persisted in the compound.[9] They even ventured to declare which elementary property predominated in a particular compound. Hence the age-old dispute is not *whether*
the elements persist in the compound, but *how* they
persist. And the "how" is reducible to the single
question, How can a compound be one being? And
this again is identical with the question, What is
the difference between a mixture and a compound?
All grant that a mixture, as sand and sugar, consists of many beings; whereas a compound, as an
animal, is one being. But how can a plurality of
elements be one being? Aristotle, in one place at
least, refuses to answer the "how," for he says,
"Whether the elements are in the compound actually
or potentially is still in dispute."[10] St. Thomas
answers that the elements are in the compound not
actually but "virtually." He explains that by the
term "virtually" he means that the characteristic
properties of the elements do not altogether cease
in the compound, they are not simply supplanted by
another and totally different set, but instead they
modify one another according to their ratio, and in
this state of mutual modification they form the

[9] Cf., e.g., St. Th., *De quattuor oppositis,* c.5; *De mixtione elementorum, ad fin.*
[10] *De coelo* III. 3.

proper equipment of one complete being, of one supposit. The elements are not *in actu*.[11] The only
being *in actu* is the whole compound, for to be *in
actu* is to be complete.[12] Some later writers, discussing how several elements can form one individual, have required a fusion of the quantity of the
components, so that the compound is said to be one
continuous, though heterogeneous, quantity of matter. These writers do not consider that hetero-
geneity is incompatible with continuity; and if rightly
explained the two are not incompatible. But the
difficulty is in verifying the continuity of inorganic
matter.

THE INDIVIDUAL IN INORGANIC MATTER. While it is
true that we recognize individual bodies as distinct by reason
of their quantity—by the fact that one is here and another
there, though they be alike in every other respect—still our
observation can never be so minute as to show us that each
individual is continuous within itself. By what means then
do we come to know a body as individual? It seems sufficient to know that (1) the constituent parts so interact
upon and modify one another as to form a *complete natural
unit*, (2) in which unit all the parts concur as a *single
principle*, (3) of a new and *specific activity*.[13] Thus we
say that an object, whether amoeba or molecule, is one being
if we see (1) that its structure is an integer. The fact that
innumerable molecules are exact replicas of one another
makes it certain that the number, kind and· order of the
parts are determined by nature, and that they form a complete natural unit. (2) We notice a unity of activity, in
the sense that the unit holds together and maintains its

---

[11] Cf. *De mixtione elementorum; In Boet. de Trin.* IV. 3 ad 6.
[12] Cf. In 2 *Sent.* D. XII, q.1, a.4 (*corp*).
[13] Cf. Palmieri, *Cosmol.*, p. 112.

structure, and at the same time acts outwardly as a single agent. (3) All the individuals must belong to the same species. They must present some characteristic property which they all have. According to these three tests each isolated molecule qualifies as an individual of inorganic matter. Atoms lose their individuality in the molecule, as the proton and electron lose theirs in the atom; because the moment anything is reduced to the status of a part it ceases to be a supposit. Some also hold that molecules lose their individuality in the crystal, which then becomes the supposit.

RÉSUMÉ. We have thus far reviewed the historical basis of the theory of matter and form, and the difficulties which the theory has encountered. The difficulties are two: the failure of the principal ancient proof for the physical distinctness of matter and form, and the difficulty of explaining the evident unity of compounds. In connection with the first it should be noted that if the matter is distinct from the form in the elements it is also distinct from the form it compounds. We shall employ another argument to prove the distinction in both cases.[14] The second difficulty is merely one of explanation, and it remains whether form be distinct from matter or not. We have shown in the previous paragraph that the explanation offered by the Scholastics does not encounter any obstacle in the most recent data of modern science. These two difficulties have occasioned much confusion of mind which in some quarters has brought the theory

[14] It must not be thought that any doubt about the physical distinctness of matter and form in the irrational world affects in any way the certainty about the physical distinctness between soul and body in man. This last psychology establishes on other and incontestable grounds.

of matter and form into disrepute. In any case a right understanding of them is necessary to a correct grasp of the state of the question. In so far as the difficulties require a concise answer we shall reserve that for replies of objections.

STATE OF THE QUESTION. The proposition which we are setting out to prove is that all bodies are composed of two essential physical parts. In other words, we have to show that substantial form is not physically identical with mere matter, that antecedently to the mind's consideration the two are not the same thing. This means, of course, that each is an *incomplete substance*. The two together make a complete substance. We contend, therefore, that substance may be a part, and still be substance. A man's arm is substance, but as a human being the arm is *incomplete*, because it is only a part. All the integral parts of a body are substance, and if substance and part were incompatible, extended bodies were impossible. It is not, however, about integral parts that we are concerned in the present thesis, but about essential parts. These essential parts are substance, and, because they are parts, are incomplete substances. Thus the soul of man is an essential part and an incomplete substance. Briefly, then, we maintain that all bodies have two essential physical parts, primary matter and substantial form.

SUBSTANTIAL FORM. Form, in the most general sense, is that which gives a thing a particular character, as the shape of a statue. Form specifies, it puts a thing in a certain class. Without form a thing is indeterminate. Forms are either accidental or substantial. *Substantial form is that substantial determinant of matter which gives matter a specific nature.* Substantial form is not here defined in such a way that its physical distinctness from primary matter is essential to the definition. We merely take cognizance of the fact that matter as we experience it in our daily lives has a variety of specific natures, and we define substantial form as that which makes matter so, whether or not form be physically distinct from any other substantial component of the bodies in question. The activities of bodies are specific, and we denominate as substantial form the prime source of those activities.[15] Certainly the form in inorganic bodies is not vital nor rational, and it is extended throughout the body. We must not, however, understand the substantial form to be the external figure or the structure of the body. It is true that we often recognize a species by reason of the structure. This structure is the effect of the substantial form; it may even be its formal effect and therefore an infallible index of the species. The structure is in that case a property or *proprium* of the substance, and hence inseparable from it; nevertheless the structure is in itself an accident, just as the specific activities are in themselves accidents; the form is the substantial source or principle of both specific structure and specific activities. Besides calling this substantial determinant of bodies the "form," Aristotle calls it also the "species," the "actuation of the matter," and "energy."

PRIMARY MATTER. In our definition of primary

[15] As a consequence, form is the source of final activities and of the physical laws.

matter it will be sufficient, previous to the proof, conceptually to distinguish it from substantial form and from the characters associated with the form. Aristotle's first definition of primary matter is: "That ultimate underlying substantial constituent of every body at which decomposition must stop, since to decompose it were to annihilate it." [16] It stands to reason that in analyzing the constituents of bodies we must come at last to something that is ultimate. If you say that this ultimate is the substantial form, since that form is the prime source of the properties, we answer that the form is the source of the *specific* properties, not of those which are *common* to all bodies. One thing common to all bodies is extension, and the subject of extension is in concept distinct from the particular substantial form of any given body. Again, we can destroy species, as is done in chemical decomposition. Now, whether you say that these are only surface changes or changes that go very deep, there must at any rate be some point at which, as Aristotle says, the changes must stop; otherwise you must say that the entire previous being was wiped out of existence, and another being sprang full-fledged from nothing into its place. There must be an ultimate subject in which these changes take place, and which remains throughout the changes. Aristotle indeed supposed that elements transmuted one another. While we cannot accept that as an experimental fact, we must admit that such change is conceivable, and in such change that substantial something which passes over from one form to another—that is, primary matter.

[16] *Phys.* I. 9. *ad fin.*

Thus matter and form are conceived as two essential parts of every material substance, and while one form may give way in favor of another, the mere matter as such is indestructible. Prime matter may be said to have integral parts but not essential parts; it is the last barrier to dissolution and one step from total annihilation.

Aristotle again defines primary matter thus: "By matter I mean that which is neither in itself a particular thing nor a certain quantity nor assigned to any other of the categories by which being is determined." [17] This is the famous negative definition. By denying that primary matter is a "particular thing" Aristotle means that it is not a complete substance. He next denies that it is identical with the accident extension as he was at pains to show in a few sentences preceding the definition. While primary matter is the root-source of extension, it is substance and in no sense an accident. Lastly it is said that prime matter has no part in determining to which species a body belongs. That is clear enough because matter is a thing common to all species of bodies.

UNION OF MATTER AND FORM. Primary matter and substantial form are not to be regarded as two supposits acting together as efficient causes, neither as coördinate principle causes, nor as principal and instrumental. Prime matter is the material cause, and substantial form is the formal cause, of the entire natural body. By an intimate communication of one to the other, they coalesce into *one supposit,* one complete substance, one nature. The complete substance is called "informed matter," or "second matter,"

---

[17] *Metaph.* VII (VI). 3, Oxford trans.

or simply "a body." No one claims that prime matter or
an inorganic form ever exists separately, each by itself. They
are always united in a body. But it is sometimes asked
whether we know bodies at all except as active forces. We
reply that a body makes itself known by *means* of active
forces, still the thing *known* is not merely force. For besides
knowing matter as something active we also know it as
something extended. Hence when Palmieri says, "Substance
is essentially a force," [18] our objection is that his statement
does not declare the *entire nature* of substance as *applied to
bodies*. Bodies present themselves not only as active but as
extended. And of these two characteristics, extension, being
common, is rightly associated with the matter, whereas active
forces, being specific, are associated with the form. Thus
the union of matter and form gives us the quantified active
substance which we call a body. In this union the form is
called the "actuation" of prime matter. An actuation, or
actus, is in general any complement which rounds out, com-
pletes or perfects a being. Form is called the *first* actuation
of matter because it is that substantial perfection which gives
matter a specific nature, and is therefore something distinct
from accidents, which are called second actuations.

SUBSTANTIAL CHANGE. Do we admit substantial change? We most decidedly do. Substantial
change is readily accepted by scientists. Chemistry
is the science of such changes. Professor A. Smith,
for example, says that "when a material changes its
properties, it has, in so doing, become a *new substance.*" Again, "The material forming one or more
substances, without ceasing to exist, may be changed
into one or more *entirely different substances.*" [19]
There is no reason why philosophy should quarrel

[18] *Cosmol.,* p. 111.
[19] *College Chemistry,* 2nd edit., p. 7.

with these statements. Specific properties flow from
the essence; hence a change of these properties
means a change of essence, and that is a substantial
change. But since the only kind of substantial
change which could clearly prove the physical distinctness of matter and form in inorganic bodies is
the now discredited transmutation of elements, we
do not use substantial change as an argument for
our thesis.

THE ARGUMENT FROM EXTENSION AND ACTIVITY.
Aristotelians of the earlier day were satisfied about
the transmutation of elements, and so did not ener-
getically seek any other proof for the physical distinction of matter and form. Avicenna, however,
did explicitly use the argument from extension and
activity.[20] Others alluded to it with approval, as
St. Bonaventure,[21] St. Thomas,[22] Suarez.[23] In this
argument we neglect all questions of substantial
changes, specific differences and particular supposits.
We can therefore be silent about these vexed questions, since their solution in no way affects the argument. We argue from the universal characteristics
of all bodies, namely, extension and activity, and
from these we draw the conclusion that every body
must ultimately be composed of two essential parts,
one the principle of its extension, the other the principle of its activity. That the former principle is
rightly called the matter, and the latter the form,
follows from the character of the two principles.

[20] *Metaph.* L.2, T.2.
[21] *Sent.* L.2, D.13, a.2, q.1.
[22] *De coelo et mundo* I. 6.
[23] *Disp. metaph.* D.13, s.10, nn.8, 10, 11.

OPPONENTS OF THE THESIS. *Atomistic philosophers,* who ignore formal cause and hence substantial form, are indirect adversaries of the thesis. Many others employ the terms matter and form in senses widely divergent, and few philosophers nowadays outside of Scholastic circles concern themselves about the real distinction.

Thesis 19. That primary matter, even in inorganic bodies, is not merely conceptually but also physically distinct from substantial form appears to follow from the nature of extension and activity

Argument. Extension is a purely passive entity and of itself is indifferent to division; force is active and effects cohesion. But these two properties are so opposite that they cannot be founded in the same ultimate substantial principle. They must in other words arise from two principles which are in some manner physically distinct. Therefore extension and force indicate that the two ultimate substantial principles of material substance are physically distinct, that matter and form are the physically twofold principles of all bodies.

The major. By saying that extension is a passive entity we mean that it does not of itself imply activity. Although bodies as we experience them resist division with greater or less force, that resistance has no relation to the extension, for different materials of the same extent resist differently. Again, division in no way destroys extension; as much extension remains after the division as before. Consequently extension is of itself totally indifferent to division.

Force produces changes, it is by its very nature efficient, active; and it retains its aptitude for action even when it is idle. There is moreover one force in bodies which can hardly be said ever to be idle, and that is the force of coherence of atoms and molecules; it varies in different bodies and in the same body under different conditions, but there is no body which does not display it in some degree.

The minor. There is opposition between such passivity and activity; and if extension as such were active, then activity in bodies should increase with their extent, which is certainly not the case. Now two opposites cannot be accounted for by an identical physical source, otherwise the properties of bodies could never reveal anything about their inner nature. Extension offers divisibility; its contribution to material substance is partition and multipliability, and it is the same in all bodies. Cohesion, on the other hand, is diametrically opposed to divisibility, and is different in different bodies. Since properties emanate from the substantial essence, the ultimate principles of these opposite properties cannot be physically identical. Therefore the physical essence of bodies consists of two parts, matter and form.

Difficulties. 1. The transmutation of elements is not supported by modern physics.

Reply. The failure of a particular argument does not disprove the thesis.

2. The ancients had great difficulty in explaining the unity of compounds.

Reply. That difficulty is not removed, but rather increased if we suppose no physical distinction between matter and form.

3. There is no incomplete substance. A thing is either a substance or it is not. It cannot be partly a substance and partly not.[24]

Reply. I grant that a thing is either a substance or not a substance, i.e., it is either a substance or an accident. It cannot be half and half. But I deny that that is what we mean by incomplete substance. What we designate as an incomplete substance is truly substance and in no sense an accident. By "incomplete" we mean that it is a part of some whole and complete substance, in other words a part of a supposit. Just as in the case of integral parts, e.g., a man's hand or foot, the fact of being part does not militate against their being substance, so also essential physical parts, e.g., soul and body, may be parts without ceasing to be substance.[25]

Topics for Discussion. Common chemical change as opposed to radioactivity. Material and formal causes. Could primary matter exist without substantial form? (Cf. Suarez, *Metaph. disput.* D. 13, sect. 4, § 9). Actuality and potency.

REFERENCES

Berthoud, A. *New Theories of Matter and the Atom* (esp. "Cohesive Energy," p. 71).

[24] Palmieri, *Ontologia,* Th. XIV.
[25] In justice to Palmieri it should be stated that, in later life, he ably answered his own objection by adducing positive evidence for the substantial union of soul and body as two incomplete substances in one supposit. (Cf. *De creatione* (1910), p. 277.)

Cath. Ency. "Matter."
Cath. World. Vol. 21, pp. 97, 234. "Matter and Form."
Harper, J. *Metaphysics of the Schools.*
Miller, L. *History of Philosophy,* No. 201.
New Scholasticism, Vol. 1, p. 297. "Theories of Matter."
O'Neill, J. *Cosmology,* Chs. 5, 6.
Perrier, J. *Revival of Scholastic Philosophy,* Ch. 4.
Thought, Vol. 1, p. 237. "Peripatetic Matter and Form."

BIBLIOGRAPHY

English

ANDRADE, E. *The Structure of the Atom* (Bell, Lond.)

BASCHAB, C. *Manual of Neo-Scholastic Philosophy* (Herder)

BOHR, N. *Theory of Spectra and Atomic Constitution* (Macmillan)

BRAGG, W. *X Rays and Crystal Structure* (Bell, Lond.)

DUBRAY, C. *Introductory Philosophy* (Longmans)

HARRIS, C. *Duns Scotus* (Oxford Press, N. Y.), Vol. 2

HARPER, J. *Metaphysics of the Schools* (Macmillan)

MAXWELL, CLERK. *Matter and Motion* (S. P. C. K., Lond.)

MERCIER, CARD. *Manual of Modern Scholastic Philosophy* (Herder), "Cosmology" by Canon Nys

MORE, L. *The Limitations of Science* (Constable, Lond.)

O'NEILL, J. *Cosmology* (Longmans)

RYAN, J. *Introduction to Philosophy* (Macmillan)

SHALLO, M. *Lessons in Scholastic Philosophy* (Reilly, Phila.)

THOMAS, ST. *Summa theologica* (Benziger), Part I

Latin

ALBERTUS MAGNUS. *De coelo et mundo. De generatione et corruptione*

BACKER, S. DE. *Institutiones metaphysicae specialis* (Delhomme et Briguet, Paris)

CONGRESSUS THOMISTICI PRIMI, *Acta*

DARIO, J. *Praelectiones cosmologicae* (G. Beauchesne, Paris)

DE MARIA. *Philosophia peripatetico-scholastica* (Fonzani, Roma), Vol. 2

DONAT, J. *Cosmologia* (Rauch, Innsbruck)

FRANK, C. *Philosophia naturalis* (Herder)

FRANZELIN, B. *Questiones selectae* (Rauch, Innsbruck)

GREDT, J. *Elementa philosophiae Aristotelico-Thomisticae* (Herder), Vol. 2

GRUENDER, H. *De qualitatibus sensibilibus* (Herder)

HAAN, H. *Philosophia naturalis* (Herder)

HICKEY, J. *Summula philosophiae* (Gill, Dublin), Vol. 2

HUGON, E. *Cursus philosophiae thomisticae* (Lethielleux, Paris), Vol. 2

LAHOUSSE, G. *Praelectiones metaphysicae specialis* (Peter, Louvain)

LEMAIRE, J. *Philosophia mineralium*

LIBERATORE, M. *Metaphysica specialis*

MENDIVE, J. *Cosmologia*

MONACO, N. *Praelectiones metaphysicae specialis* (Typ. Pontif., Roma), Pars 1

PALMIERI, D. *Institutiones philosophicae,* Vol. 2

PESCH, T. *Philosophia naturalis* (Herder)

SAN, L. DE. *Institutiones metaphysicae specialis* (Fonteyn, Louvain)

SCHAAF, H. *Institutiones cosmologiae* (Giachetti, Roma)

SCHIFFINI, S. *Disputationes metaphysicae specialis* (Speirani, Turin), Vol. 1

SUAREZ, F. *Metaphysicae disputationes,* D. 12-54

THOMAS, ST. *Summa theologica, I. Summa contra gentiles. De coelo et mundo. De generatione et corruptione,* I, c. 1-17. *De mixtione elementorum. De aeternitate mundi. De quattuor oppositis,* c. 5

TONGIORGI, S. *Institutiones philosophicae,* Vol. 2

URRÁBURU, J. *Institutiones philosophicae: cosmologia. Philosophia naturalis.* Compendium, Vol. 3

VAN DER AA. *Praelectionum conspectus* (Fonteyn, Louvain), Vol. 3

VAISSIÈRE, J. DE LA. *Cursus philosophiae naturalis* (Beauchesne, Paris)

French

DESCOQS, P. *Essai critique sur l'hylémorphisme* (Beauchesne, Paris)

DUHEM, P. *Le mixte et la combinaison chemique* (Naud, Paris)
Le système du monde (Hermann, Paris)

NYS, D. *Cosmologie* (Louvain U.)

RENOIRTE, F. *La critique Einsteinienne* (Louvain U.)

TONQUÉDEC, J. DE. *Introduction a l'étude du merveilleux et du miracle* (Beauchesne, Paris)

German

GATTERER, A. *Das Problem des stat. Naturgesetzes* (Rauch, Innsbruck)

GEYSER, J. *Naturerkenntnis und Kausalgesetz* (Schöningh, Münster)

GUTBERLET, C. *Naturphilosophie* (Theissing, Münster)

HAGEN, J. *"Dunkle Nebel und Sternleeren"* (*Astr. Nach.* 1921)

KLIMKE, F. *Der Monismus* (Herder)

PESCH, T. *Die grossen Welträtsel* (Herder)

POHLE, J. *Die Sternenwelten und ihre Bewohner* (Bachem, Köln)

UDE, J. *Monistische oder teleologische Weltanschauung*

INDEX

Absolute, in modern monism, 49.
Abstraction, in mathematics, 82.
Accidents, proper and contingent (or logical), 87.
Action at a distance, 81, 137.
Activity, definition, 131; immanent and transient, 135; and extension, universal characteristics of bodies, 227.
Actuation of matter, 226.
Affinity (chemical) unexplained in atomism, 193.
Alexander, S., on space-time, 50.
Allotropic forms, definition, 217.
Ampère, dynamist, 82.
Anaxagoras, on other human races, 9; purpose, 19.
Anaxamander, on evolution, 33.
Appetite, merely natural, 18; elicited, 18; sensitive, 18; rational, 18.
Aristotle, on teleology, 19; preexistence of matter, 29; beginning of world, 46; definition of extension, 61; quantity, 87; place, 104; definition of time, 111; of activity, 131; criticism of Democritus, 151; atomism, 186, 188; atoms, 197; substantial form, 199; cause of specific properties, 202; Atomists and Eleatics, 214; ice the element water; 217; elements in compound, 219; names for substantial form, 223; definition of prime matter (positive), 224, (negative), 225.
Arrhenius, on restoration of energy, 40.

Artificial bodies, definition, 14, 146.
Atomism, scientific, 183; philosophical, 183; definition, 184; and change, 185; materialistic, 188; mechanical, 189; insufficient to explain matter, 194; opposed to substantial form, 197.
Atoms, quantitative units, 184; of energy, 190; not like solar system, 194; and Aristotle, 197.
Attribute, a common property, 138.
Augustine, St., on evolution, 32; time, 109.
Averroes, opposed to atomism, 186.
Avicenna, and atomism, 186; proof of hylomorphism, 227.

Bacon, Francis, omits purpose, 19; and atomism, 186.
Ball, R., 31.
Balmes, J., 57; and continuum, 63; Dynamist, 82.
Baschab, C., 86.
Bauer, B., on miracles, 165.
Bayma, Dynamist, 82; on space, 100.
Bergson, on time, 114; simultaneity, 124; organicism, 187.
Berthoud, A., on matter, 134, 190; mistaken about ancient elements, 217.
Body, descriptive and essential definitions, 92.
Bodies, and time, 121; natural, 146; artificial, 146.

237